ENDANGERED SPECIES

James M. Dunn
Ben E. Loring
Phil D. Strickland

All royalties on
this book will go to
the World Hunger Fund of
the Foreign Mission Board of
the Southern Baptist Convention

Broadman Press
Nashville, Tennessee

4261-17
ISBN: 0-8054-6117-5

Dewey Decimal Classification: 261.832
Subject headings: FOOD SUPPLY//CHURCH AND SOCIAL PROBLEMS
Library of Congress Catalog Card No.: 76-27481

Foreword

There has been a tragic and unbiblical separation between witnessing to the good news of Christ and acting with his love to meet human need. How dare we present Christ as the Bread of life to a hungry man and only be concerned with Christ as the spiritual bread, and not obey Christ by providing the physical bread to meet that man's physical needs of today.

As Christians we have the motivation of the love of God, which cannot be duplicated by government or other secular approaches to the world food problem. I suggest that pastors and lay people alike take up the cross daily, sacrificing for others in a measurable material sense.

We all need to be aware of the great complexity of world hunger problems. The staff of the Christian Life Commission for Texas Baptists has done a splendid service in this regard by offering us an opportunity through this book to learn more of the needs and how we may respond.

MARK O. HATFIELD

Acknowledgments

This book has actually been a team effort by the staff of the Christian Life Commission of the Baptist General Convention of Texas. The Commission has given us encouragement and support. The executive secretary of the Baptist General Convention of Texas, Dr. James H. Landes, has been understanding and helpful as we have done our work.

The book would not have been possible without Tony Martin's research, the diligent help of Rita Armentrout and Nancy Carson, and the dedicated editing and checking of the manuscript by Lou Milstead. We are also indebted to our families for their patience and affirmation.

We offer this book and any royalties that may come from it to the cause of meeting world hunger needs. It is our prayer that God will use this effort to sensitize consciences and inform caring Christians.

James M. Dunn
Ben E. Loring, Jr.
Phil D. Strickland

Contents

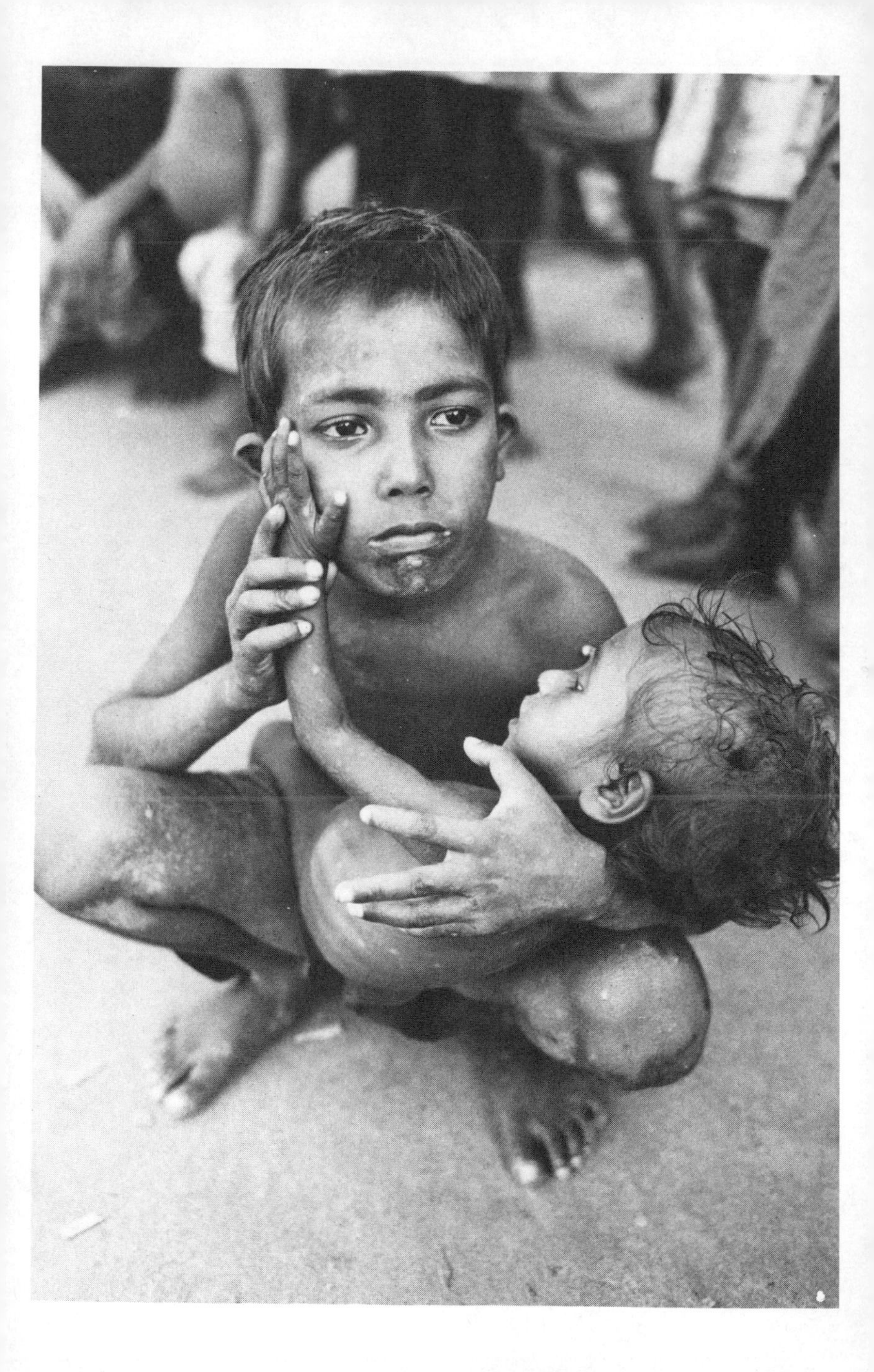

1
Can You Show Me a Picture of Hunger?

World Hunger. The words may conjure up various pictures in your mind: small children with distended stomachs, homeless multitudes in teeming refugee camps, aged persons with spindly bodies, emaciated corpses stacked in funeral pyres. Whatever the image may be, it cannot be a pleasant sight.

The tragedy of world hunger is people who are starving, not a cosmic piece of dust called the earth. World hunger is not a picture of a globe anxious to be fed but rather a picture of people who urgently need the necessity of life—food.

World hunger is nomads in Chad forced to eat leaves and bark to stay alive. It is two-year-old babies dying in Mauretania never weighing more than sixteen pounds. World hunger is fourteen thousand people crowded together in a refugee camp in Kebri Dehar with only two nurses. World hunger in Ethiopia is feeding the seeds saved for next year's crop to the children when they cry from hunger.

The most obvious consequence of hunger is the toll it takes in human lives. In the last two years it has been estimated that even by a conservative count over ten million persons per year are dying from starvation.

In a *Time* magazine feature on the world hunger crisis, Peter Stoler describes how hunger kills its victim.

> The victim of starvation burns up his own body fats, muscles and tissues for fuel. His body quite literally consumes itself and deteriorates rapidly. The kidneys, liver and endocrine system often cease to function properly. A shortage of carbohydrates, which play a vital role in brain

chemistry, affects the mind. Lassitude and confusion set in, so that starvation victims often seem unaware of their plight. The body's defenses drop; disease kills most famine victims before they have time to starve to death. An individual begins to starve when he has lost about a third of his normal body weight. Once this loss exceeds 40%, death is almost inevitable.[1]

The majority of these deaths caused by lack of food are children five years of age and under. The United Nations Food and Agricultural Organization estimates that an average of ten thousand children die of starvation daily.[2] Lester R. Brown, noted agronomist and economist, states:

It is the children who are often victims of malnutrition. Severely malnourished infants or children have low resistance and frequently die of routine childhood diseases. In Latin America malnutrition is the primary cause, or a major contributing factor, in 50 to 75 percent of the deaths of children aged one to four years.[3]

Stanley Mooneyham, president and founder of World Vision International, a Christian relief organization vitally involved in the lives of people around the world, helps us translate these tragic statistics into personal reality. He describes his visit with a poverty-stricken, starving family in Brazil.

In Natal, about 1,400 miles north of Sao Paulo, I sat on the dirt floor of a hovel and shared one of those dramas. In the cast were Sebastian and Maria Nascimento and their nine children. The stage was a one-room thatched lean-to, more or less divided into living and sleeping areas by a torn piece of rubber sheeting. The floor was sand. The stage props were minimal–one stool, a charcoal hibachi, four cots covered with gunny sacks filled with a thin layer of straw.

My emotions could scarcely take in what I saw and heard. The three-year-old twins, lying naked and unmoving on a small cot, were into the last act of their personal drama. Mercifully, the curtain was coming down on their brief appearance. Malnutrition was the villain. The two-year-old played a silent role, his brain already vegetating from marasmus, a severe form of malnourishment.

The father is without work. Both he and Maria are anguished over their existence, but they are too proud to beg. He tries to shine shoes. Maria cannot talk about their condition. She tries, but words just will not come. Her mother's love is deep and tender, and the daily deterioration of her children is more than she can bear. Tears must be the vocabulary of the anguished soul. I have noticed that the poor cry a lot. At such an intimate moment, my own words sound empty and hollow so I, too, choose not to speak. The drama has reached its most intense moment as it moves from words to feelings.

I have entered into the edge of their hell, but I can go no further.

As I walk out slowly through an opening in the thatch wall—there is no door—I am met by the most incongruous sight I can imagine, and I suddenly realize that what I have left is reality and what I have stepped into is fantasy. Stretched out before me is one of the most beautiful expanses of beach in Brazil. The Atlantic Ocean which washes the sand is shaded from pale green out to deep blue. It is a holiday and the beach is thronged with swimmers and surfers. The nerve ends of my emotions are still raw and hurting from my encounter with the Nascimentos, so I am shocked at the gaiety and frivolity going on below me while a struggle with death is taking place behind me.

It takes me a little while to remember that what I have seen is the story of all humanity and that most of the time I, too, am figuratively "at the beach" while the poor fight their daily survival battles. When I remember, I am ashamed.[4]

The world of reality described by Stanley Mooneyham involves horrors those of us living in the world of fantasy find difficult to believe. Lester Brown reminds us:

Severe famine is always a horror. Humans not only suffer and die in large numbers, but many are pushed to extreme behavior by starvation. In addition to hoarding and stealing food, starving people have been known to resort to murder and cannibalism as well as to selling children to obtain money for food.[5]

Such desperate action tragically answers the rhetorical question raised in Lamentations 2:20, "Should women eat their offspring, the little ones who were born healthy?" It is a reality we want to deny, but we cannot. It is a part of the tragedy we casually call "world hunger."

The hunger crisis takes its toll on human beings in other ways than the ultimate consequence of death. Mooneyham relates a visit with a mother of a starving family in Singhali. Concerning her children, he asks:

How does hunger affect their sleep?

"The children sleep whether they are hungry or not. But we hold such feelings for them and we worry so for them, that we do not get enough sleep."

Do the children cry from hunger?

Tears fill the eyes of the mother as she says: "The children cry much of the time because they are hungry. It is hard for us not to weep with them."[6]

Tears can fill the eyes of anyone who understands what prolonged hunger does to people. *Time* magazine describes the devastating impact of hunger on children who suffer but do not die as a result of too little to eat.

Children who survive starvation remain scarred for life. No amount of vitamin D will straighten legs bowed by rickets; proper portions of essential proteins cannot undo the damage done to a growing child's brain by their absence. Brain cells require protein, and they need it from the very moment that life begins. At least 80% of all human brain growth occurs between conception and the age of two. This growth cannot take place in the fetus if the mother is malnourished, and it cannot be accomplished in the infant if he is starving. Nor will it happen later. In many cases, brain development that does not occur when it is supposed to does not take place at all. Thus hunger is condemning countless thousands of infants—from Harlem to the Sahel—to the twilight zone of mental retardation and leaving them no hope of deliverance.[7]

The *Center Survey* describes the lack of energy that results from being deprived of enough food to function normally.

An undernourished individual has little mental and physical energy. This lethargic condition is often called "laziness" and cited as the cause of poverty. Actually this "laziness" is often a result of a poverty diet, rather than the cause of poverty. An undernourished "growing" child loses weight and becomes lethargic. Body growth slows or even stops. The child's ability to learn in school and/or from the various stimuli in his or her environment is seriously handicapped. When prolonged, undernourishment can cause a deficit in learning that is nearly impossible to make up, even if an adequate diet is restored.[8]

Alan Berg relates how this lethargy is reflected in the lives of persons who are plagued with malnutrition.

The light of curiosity absent from children's eyes. Twelve-year-olds with the physical stature of eight-year-olds. Youngsters who lack the energy to brush aside flies collecting about the sores on their faces. Agonizingly slow reflexes of adults crossing traffic. Thirty-year-old mothers who look sixty. All are common images in developing countries; all reflect inadequate nutrition; all have societal consequences.[9]

The inability to move normally can have tragic consequences. *Time* magazine described a famine in Ethiopia that left a hundred thousand dead in two provinces. Some of the people were so weakened by hunger that when a rainstorm struck their city, they were unable to raise their heads from the gutter. They drowned in a couple inches of water.[10]

How widespread is hunger in the world? Jane Brody states in a *New York Times* article:

Malnutrition is now epidemic in many countries. Experts estimate that nearly a third of the world's people are suffering from hunger and its consequences, and that the diets of half the world's children lack adequate protein, the nutrient most essential to proper physical and mental development.[11]

Lester Brown concurs. He says, "The silent crisis of malnutrition may be denying close to a billion human beings the basic right to realize their full potential, their full humanity."[12]

Such widespread hunger causes the far too familiar scenes of people begging for their daily sustenance. A traveler to one of the hunger-plagued countries of the world recorded in his journal his encounter with begging children. He writes: "My most vivid memory was the little girl who looked about three years old leading her blind sister, who could not have been over five years old, from car to car. Two tiny, dying children with swollen stomachs and skinny arms moving from car to car." [13]

Begging for food and being deprived of basic necessities of life can have a devastating impact on one's understanding of his own worth and value. Stan Mooneyham offers a moving example, He cites the newspaper interview of one of Bogota, Colombia's street children.

> Called "Frijolito" (little bean) because of his size, he never slept in a bed for two years. His bed was under the fountains of Bolivar Square or among the columns of the capitol building.
>
> "I passed uncountable nights awake suffering from cold and hunger. When you're hungry, cold hits harder. I waited for dawn and attacked the leftovers on the tables of the night watchmen. . . . One day I cried bitterly. In front of me a woman served warm milk to her dog. She covered him with a special wool coat. Later she served him a biscuit and bread and covered him with scented powder. He had an identification tag around his neck and a pendant and the woman took him to her chauffeur-driven car.
>
> "I was hungry, and it was obvious. I smelled bad and didn't have warm milk or a wool shirt. I discovered that my life meant less than that of a dog." [14]

It is understandable that Frijolito could draw such an evaluation of his personal worth when confronted with the life-style of the more affluent. In a world where distance is reduced dramatically by modern communications, affluent persons must deal with the impact of their life-style on the rest of the world. The newsletter of The Interreligious Foundation for Community Organization offers an analogy.

> If the world were a global village of 100 people, 70 of them would be unable to read, and only one would have a college education. Over 50 would be suffering from malnutrition, and over 80 would live in

what we call substandard housing. If the world were a global village of 100 residents, 6 of them would be Americans. These 6 would have half of the village's entire income, and the other 94 would exist on the half.[15]

The traveler mentioned earlier in this chapter notes in his journal the stark contrasts he observed between the hungry nations and the United States.

The contrasts were immediate and vivid: skinny people instead of plump people, dirty people (few bath facilities and little water) instead of clean people, huts instead of homes, walking instead of riding, sick people instead of healthy people, fires instead of electricity, weak people instead of strong people, agriculture instead of industry, poverty instead of wealth, rags instead of suits, hungry people instead of satiated people.[16]

Those of us who have enough to eat have difficulty identifying emotionally with the world's hungry people. Diogenes, the Greek philosopher, when asked when was the proper time to eat, replied: "If a rich man, when you will; if a poor man, when you can."

Too many of us are arguing about hunger on a full stomach As the world's people starve, we watch them starve on color television.

As we begin to realize the radical difference between the average residents of the developed nations and the impoverished in the rest of the world, the inevitable question arises, What do we do about it? Some pessimistic persons have made the suggestion that we take the radical approach known as *triage.*

Triage is a battlefield term that was used during World War I. Because of the high number of casualties and the inadequate supply of medical personnel in field hospitals, a system evolved to determine who would be treated. This system was known as triage.

The wounded were divided into three categories on the basis

of their potential for survival. One group was composed of wounded who would survive without immediate medical attention. Another group included those who more than likely would die even with adequate medical care. The third group were the persons who might live if properly treated. It was this third group who received the concentrated efforts of the medical team. Only when they were cared for would any medical attention be given to the other two groups.

It is the suggestion of a number of scholars that a triage approach be taken concerning the problem of world hunger. They are saying: "Since many are going to starve to death anyway, why should we help them? Let's concentrate our resources on only those who have the best chance of survival."

The triage concept may make good medical sense on the battlefield, but it is morally outrageous when it is applied to the hunger needs of suffering humanity. Nevin S. Scrimshaw, professor at Massachusetts Institute of Technology, says that the triage approach to the world hunger problem is wrong because it is based on three assumptions that are globally false.[17]

First, triage assumes that the present situation is beyond our ability to help. Nevin Scrimshaw says this is not true. He points out that we responded to an urgent food crisis following World War II. The resources are available if we decide to muster them.

Secondly, triage assumes that if we do help now, it will lead to worse problems in the future. Nevin Scrimshaw responds by pointing out that this assumption ignores the "emergency" nature of the present food crisis. Much of the current food shortage has been caused by a number of unusual climatic changes combined with a temporary shortage of fertilizer, seed grains, and other aspects vital to the food-producing process.

Finally, Scrimshaw says that the triage proposal assumes a straight-line projection of present resources. It does not take into account any new development possibilities. He insists that much progress is being made in such areas as birth control, agricultural development, and other areas that will dramatically affect the balance between food and population.

From a Christian perspective, triage is an unacceptable approach to the world food crisis because it does not take into account the inherent worth and value of every human being. The fact that all persons are made in the image of God determines that every member of the human family is of equal value. Therefore, everything possible must be done to meet the needs of all. Triage is morally unacceptable from a Christian perspective.

The Greek philosopher Aristotle once described the human condition in this way, "From time to time, it is necessary that pestilence, famine, and war prune the luxuriant growth of the human race." *Newsweek* magazine commented on his quote by saying, "And so it may be–for it is not at all clear that mankind has mellowed enough to allow a more civilized set of ethics to prevail." [18]

It is the assumption of this book that in Christ a new ethic prevails. If we can apply adequately the teachings of our Lord to the current phenomenon of world hunger, we believe there can be positive solutions offered. It requires that we take an honest look at the Scriptures, our theology, and the nature of the hunger crisis and our role in it. It means that we must be willing to reevaluate and reconstruct our life-styles. As we do so, we can become like the early Christians who were defended in the court of Roman Emperor Hadrian (A.D. 117-138) by a non-Christian named Aristides. He offered this description. May it be true of us.

Christians love one another. They never fail to help widows; they save orphans from those who would hurt them. If a man has something, he freely gives to the man who has nothing. If they see a stranger, Christians take him home and are happy, as though he were a real brother. . . . If one of them is poor and there isn't enough food to go around, they fast several days to give him the food he needs. . . . This is really a new kind of person. There is something divine in them.

For Thought and Discussion

1. What do you think of when the words *world hunger* are mentioned? What feelings do you have when the issue is discussed? Can these feelings be altered? Why or why not?

2. What is it like to be hungry? What is the difference between being hungry and starving to death? Imagine what it would be like to see your family members dying from starvation. Describe it.

3. What is the concept of triage? How has it been applied to the problem of world hunger? Evaluate triage from a Christian perspective.

4. What are the crucial factors concerning our role in the world hunger crisis? How can we become more "Christian" in our response to the issue?

2
You Mean There's a Verse in the Bible About Bangladesh?

People have been hungry throughout history. The Bible indicates a profound awareness of the problem of human hunger. As Christians face the contemporary ravages of this ancient enemy, we would do well to heed the biblical insights and admonitions concerning our responsibility to hungry people. Both the Old and New Testaments speak to the hunger problem with shocking clarity and challenging suggestions. A synopsis of the Bible's teaching concerning hungry people can be categorized under five consistent biblical themes.

1. *Hungry people are a special concern of the heavenly Father.* God's compassion for people who are hungry is revealed in the Bible in various ways. Some of the most explicit demonstrations of this compassion are found in the law codes of the Old Testament. In these practical instructions to the people of Israel, God makes special provision for the hungry.

> Now when you reap the harvest of your land, you shall not reap to the very corners of your field, neither shall you gather the gleanings of your harvest. Nor shall you glean your vineyard, nor shall you gather the fallen fruit of your vineyard; you shall leave them for the needy and the stranger. I am the Lord your God (Lev. 19:9-10).[1]

These instructions are repeated again in Deuteronomy 24:19-22.

> When you reap your harvest in your field and have forgotten a sheaf in the field, you shall not go back to get it; it shall be for the alien, for the orphan, and for the widow, in order that the Lord your God

may bless you in all the work of your hands. When you beat your olive tree, you shall not go over the boughs again; it shall be for the alien, for the orphan, and for the widow. When you gather the grapes of your vineyard, you shall not go over it again; it shall be for the alien, for the orphan, and for the widow. And you shall remember that you were a slave in the land of Egypt; therefore I am commanding you to do this thing.

It is important to note that in both of these explicit directions concerning the harvest of crops, the admonition to leave portions of the crops in the field for the hungry is given under strong reminders of God's authority and activity in their lives. The Leviticus 19 passage closes with the solemn reminder, "I am the Lord." The final verse in Deuteronomy 24 recalls the fact that the one who issues these commands is the same one who freed them from oppression in Egypt. Clearly the rules for harvesting crops are given with the divine intention that all people, including the hungry, might be cared for by the productivity of the land. Obedience to these laws is motivated by the awareness that they are a reflection of the character and holiness of God. The laws are indications of how God deals with all persons and, therefore, how individuals must deal with one another. Leviticus 19:2 declares, "You shall be holy, for I the Lord your God am holy."

In other Old Testament passages God further identifies himself as being on the side of the poor who are the hungry and dispossessed. In Isaiah 3:15, he refers to them as "My people." His compassion for the hungry causes him to be active on their behalf. Proverbs 22:22-23 warns:

Do not rob the poor because he is poor,
Or crush the afflicted at the gate;
For the Lord will plead their case,
And take the life of those who rob them.

God's advocacy on the behalf of the helpless and hungry is

"Give us this day..."

also depicted in Psalm 140:12, "I know that the Lord will maintain the cause of the afflicted, and justice for the poor."

In addition to God's defense of the hungry, he also is described as the one who provides food for those in need.

> How blessed is he whose God is the God of Jacob,
> Whose hope is in the Lord his God.
> Who executes justice for the oppressed;
> Who gives food to the hungry (Ps. 146:5,7).

God acts as benefactor to those who are hungry because of the anguish of their wretched condition. Lamentations 4:9-10 describes the tragedy of the hunger stricken.

> Better are those slain with the sword
> Than those slain with hunger;
> For they pine away, being stricken
> For the lack of the fruits of the field.
> The hands of compassionate women
> Boiled their own children;
> They became food for them
> Because of the destruction of the daughter of my people.

The desperate condition of the starving and stricken moves the Lord to divine intervention on their behalf. "Because of the devastation of the afflicted, because of the groaning of the needy, Now I will arise," says the Lord; "I will set him in the safety for which he longs" (Ps. 12:5).

God identifies himself with the poor to such a degree that an individual's reaction to the poor is understood as his attitude toward the Lord. Proverbs 14:31 declares: "He who oppresses the poor reproaches his Maker, But he who is gracious to the needy honors Him." Proverbs 17:5 contains a similar admonition: "He who mocks the poor reproaches his Maker; he who rejoices at calamity will not go unpunished." To minister to a poor and hungry person is in fact ministry unto the Lord. "He who is gracious to a poor man lends to the Lord, and He will repay him for his good deed" (Prov. 19:17).

These random admonitions and specific dictates clearly reveal a God who is biased on the behalf of the poor and hungry. According to the Bible, hungry people are a special concern of the heavenly Father.

2. *Food is understood as a basic human right.* The importance of food to the sustenance of life is assumed in the Scriptures. The word "bread" appears 321 times in the Revised Standard Version while the word "eat" appears 420 times.[2] The multiplicity of these occurrences simply underscores the acceptance of food as vital to the process of human living. To be without food is to be deprived of a basic human right.

The law code of the Old Testament as recorded in Leviticus and Deuteronomy sought to provide basic food needs for all persons, even the beggar, the destitute, and the alien sojourner. These laws, relating to harvesting of crops, took into account the necessity of food for every individual. More important than the profit that might be earned from the sale of every scrap of harvestable food was the provision of basic necessities of life to the hungry and dispossessed.

The basic human right of food is emphasized in the model prayer of Jesus. At the heart of his petition to the Father, Jesus prays, "Give us this day our daily bread" (Matt. 6:11). The inclusion of this request for food necessary to daily sustenance indicates that the incarnate God understands the life necessities of his creation. Dean Freudenberger and Paul Minus identify some vital lessons the Lord's Prayer teaches us concerning food as a basic human right.

> When we seek the meaning of this portion of the Lord's Prayer in relation to the total biblical faith, we discover fresh horizons opened for our thinking and acting at four principal points. It helps us understand (1) that God has created the entire universe in such a way that it can provide every person with the food necessary for a full life;

(2) that hunger results from our disrupting the intended order of God's creation; (3) that God has acted in Jesus Christ to free the creation from the forces that keep the human family from responsibly using and sharing his gifts; and (4) that the church is called to spearhead the extension of Christ's liberating work to the whole creation in every age.[3]

As Freudenberger and Minus correctly point out, God has created the world in such a way that the food needs of the human family are provided for when the food-producing process continues in accord with his intention. Our petitioning the Father for basic necessities of life reminds us of our total dependence upon him.

God's understanding of the importance of food to human existence is illustrated graphically in the account of the miracle of the feeding of the multitude by Jesus. It is the only miracle performed during the ministry of Jesus that is recorded in all four Gospels. The Master's provision of food to the multitude signaled his awareness of the necessity of daily food while demonstrating his capacity to meet total human need.

The most extensive report of the miracle of the feeding of the five thousand by our Lord is contained in the sixth chapter of the Gospel of John. In this passage the Gospel writer includes not only the account of the miracle but also an analysis from our Lord of the meaning of the miracle. Jesus, the morning following the miracle event, enters into a dialogue with a representative group of persons who had been fed the day before. In this discussion Jesus identified himself as the "bread of life" (John 6:35,48,51). He continues with the illustration to say that he is also the meat and the drink of life.

Jesus therefore said to them, "Truly, truly, I say to you, unless you eat the flesh of the Son of Man and drink His blood, you have no life in yourselves. He who eats My flesh and drinks My blood has eternal life; and I will raise him up on the last day. For My flesh is true food and My blood is true drink. He who eats My flesh and drinks My blood abides in Me, and I in him" (John 6:53-56).

The analogy Jesus offers is a powerful one. He is taking a basic life need, the requirement of physical food for physical life, and illustrating the deepest need within the human personality, the need for relationship with God which only he can provide. Jesus is saying that just as food is absolutely vital to human existence, so he is vital to life itself. To be without food is to starve; to be without Jesus is to be empty of life; "you have no life in yourselves." To partake of bread, meat, and drink is to sustain physical life; to partake of him is to find life abundant and eternal. It is an analogy with which any human being can identify.

As we consider the depth of human spiritual need and the ability of Jesus to meet that need, we commit heresy if we fail to see the affirmation Jesus makes concerning the importance of food. He does not disregard the necessity of daily food. Rather, he acknowledges the food need of every individual and in so doing communicates his offering of himself to meet the equally vital spiritual needs of life. In words and actions Jesus dramatically affirms food as a basic human right.

3. *Hungry people exist only as a result of human sin.* Within the scope of God's economy, God has made provision for the food needs of mankind. The earth was created with the basic capacity to produce food fit for human consumption (Gen. 1:29-30). God intended the human family to maintain the earth for the benefit of all (Gen. 1:28). God is active in the processes necessary for the continuing provision of food (Ps. 147:8).

God's intention to provide enough food for the entire human family is illustrated in the law codes of the Old Testament. His requirement to leave produce in the field for the benefit of the poor and needy illustrates his desire for all to be fed.

With these facts in mind, the inevitable question becomes,

Why are people hungry? The Bible responds with a clear answer: because of sin. The impact of sin upon the whole human family is seen most graphically in the distortion of God's intention to provide for all by the natural resources of the earth. Stuffed stomachs from obesity and bloated bellies from malnutrition testify to the tragic consequences of human sinfulness. By the manipulation and exploitation of the earth's resources to benefit a few at the expense of many, sin continues to evidence its reality among us.

The Bible speaks harsh words concerning the distortion of God's intention by those who would profit excessively from the earth's resources.

> Hear this, you who trample the needy, to do away with the humble of the land, saying, "When will the new moon be over, so that we may buy grain, and the sabbath, that we may open the wheat market to make the bushel smaller and the shekel bigger, and to cheat with dishonest scales, so as to buy the helpless for money, and the needy for a pair of sandals, and that we may sell the refuse of the wheat" (Amos 8:4-6).

The marketplace is manipulated to provide economic advantage to those who already possess abundance while the rights of the impoverished are completely ignored. The "refuse of the wheat" that was to be left in the field for the sustenance of the starving is greedily exchanged for material gain. The real effect of this inequity is to "buy the helpless for money, and the needy for a pair of sandals." The sin of placing economic priorities over human concerns is a gross distortion of God's design for the provision of all his family, resulting in tragic consequences for those in the greatest need.

The Bible condemns the sin of greed, which causes the deprivation of the needy. Amos promises harsh judgment from the Lord upon the "cows of Bashan who are on the mountain of Samaria, who oppress the poor, who crush the needy, who say to your husbands, 'Bring now, that we may drink!' " (Amos 4:1).

Ezekiel declares: "Behold, this was the guilt of your sister Sodom: she and her daughters had arrogance, abundant food, and careless ease, but she did not help the poor and needy. Thus they were haughty and committed abominations before Me. Therefore I removed them when I saw it" (Ezek. 16:49-50). Thus the judgment of God upon Sodom was not only because of sexual deviations but because even with their abundance they failed to care for the impoverished.

God's wrath upon the sin of profiteering from the impoverished and consuming the food of the hungry is dramatically declared in Isaiah 3:13-15.

> The Lord arises to contend,
> And stands to judge the people.
> The Lord enters into judgment with the elders
> and the princes of His people:
> "It is you who have devoured the vineyard;
> The plunder of the poor is in your houses.
> What do you mean by crushing My people,
> And grinding the face of the poor?"
> Declares the Lord God of hosts.

It is out of the awareness that extravagant abundance is always at the expense of those in greatest need that the Bible condemns the sin of gluttony. It is a practical evidence of the sin of greed. When the people of Israel were in the wilderness following their deliverance from Egypt, God provided for their physical sustenance by giving manna for daily consumption (Ex. 16). However, when they sought to store more than they could eat in a day, it "bred worms and became foul" (Ex. 16:20). In addition, when God met their need for meat by the provision of a flight of quails, their greediness caused a plague among them. The dead resulting from the plague were buried in a place that was to be known as the "graves of greediness" (Num. 11:34).

Gluttony is depicted as a sin that distorts God's intention to provide food for the human family. It is the acquisition of abundance by the exploitation of the earth's natural resources. The Bible promises destruction to those who follow a gluttonous life-style (Prov. 23:19-21; Amos 6:4-7, Phil. 3:19).

The Bible reveals that people are hungry and die of starvation only because of our sin. The oppression of the poor, the deprivation of the needy, and the ignoring of the hungry are defined as sin in both the Old and New Testaments. Perhaps the clearest statement of this sin is seen in the final judgment scene described by our Lord in Matthew 25. Jesus identifies himself with the hungry to the degree that our denial of food to the starving is in fact a denial of the Lord himself. He promises final judgment on those who saw him hungry and gave him nothing to eat (Matt. 25:42).

4. *God expects the righteous to meet the needs of the hungry.* The Bible accepts the presence of the poor who are hungry and needy as a permanent reality. Jesus gives evidence of this fact when he responds to the rebuke of the disciples concerning the woman who anointed him with expensive ointment. Jesus says: "The poor you always have with you, and whenever you wish, you can do them good; but you do not always have Me" (Mark 14:7).

This statement of Jesus is often quoted only as an argument to defend not helping those in need. Such emphasis is a distortion of the truth. Jesus was quoting a verse from a passage in Deuteronomy that called for ministry to the poor.

> If there is a poor man with you, one of your brothers, in any of your towns in your land which the Lord your God is giving you, you shall not harden your heart, nor close your hand from your poor brother; but you shall freely open your hand to him, and shall generously lend him sufficient for his need in whatever he lacks. Beware, lest there is a base thought in your heart, saying, 'The seventh year, the year

of remission, is near,' and your eye is hostile toward your poor brother, and you give him nothing; then he may cry to the Lord against you, and it will be a sin in you. You shall generously give to him, and your heart shall not be grieved when you give to him, because for this thing the Lord your God will bless you in all your work and in all your undertakings. For the poor will never cease to be in the land; therefore I command you, saying, 'You shall freely open your hand to your brother, to your needy and poor in your land' (Deut. 15:7-11).

It is obvious that the passage is identifying the presence of the poor as a continuing opportunity for ministry. God's children are responsible for caring for the poor, needy, and hungry. Their very presence demands ministry on their behalf from the people of God.

It is because of the continuing presence of the needy in human society that God's statutes institute a system of sharing. This system of sharing described in the law codes in Leviticus and Deuteronomy is intended to help provide for the needs of the poor and hungry. The system of sharing not only required a portion of the harvest to be left in the fields, but also it required fair wages, quick payment of wages, and generosity on the part of those with possessions.

It is the righteous who are responsible for maintaining God's system of sharing. Unjust action on the part of the people of God is rebuked while responsible action for the benefit of those in need is called for in Psalm 82:2-4.

How long will you judge unjustly,
And show partiality to the wicked?
Vindicate the weak and fatherless;
Do justice to the afflicted and destitute.
Rescue the weak and needy;
Deliver them out of the hand of the wicked.

God has promised to bless those who are faithful in meeting the needs of the deprived while he judges those who ignore the needs of the hungry.

> He who gives to the poor will never want,
> But he who shuts his eyes will have many curses
> (Prov. 28:27).

The righteous person is to be an instrument of God to relieve the suffering of the poor. Even religious functions are to help alleviate the anguish of the hungry. Isaiah 58:6-11 describes the kind of worship that is beneficial to those in need as well as the one who worships.

> Is this not the fast which I chose,
> To loosen the bonds of wickedness,
> To undo the bands of the yoke,
> And to let the oppressed go free,
> And break every yoke?
> Is it not to divide your bread with the hungry,
> And bring the homeless poor into the house;
> When you see the naked, to cover him;
> And not to hide yourself from your own flesh?
> Then your light will break out like the dawn,
> And your recovery will speedily spring forth;
> And your righteousness will go before you;
> The glory of the Lord will be your rear guard.
> Then you will call, and the Lord will answer;
> You will cry, and He will say, 'Here I am.'
> If you remove the yoke from your midst
> The pointing of the finger, and speaking wickedness,
> And if you give yourself to the hungry,
> And satisfy the desire of the afflicted,
> Then your light will rise in darkness,
> And your gloom will become like midday.
> And the Lord will continually guide you,
> And satisfy your desire in scorched places,
> And give strength to your bones;
> And you will be like a watered garden,
> And like a spring of water whose waters do not fail.

As this beautiful passage indicates, the person who finds the resources of life full as a result of his relationship with God will find opportunities of vital ministry on the behalf of those in desperate need. True worship involves relieving oppression, feeding hungry persons, and caring for human needs. By such worship the righteous enjoy the presence of God while they fulfill their responsibility to be his channels of relief.

5. *The new covenant demands more of God's people than the old covenant.* The New Testament assumes a knowledge of and commitment to a system of justice that is explicit in the Old Testament. This system of justice includes a concern for the poor and an awareness of the responsibility of the people of God to respond to human need. The majority of the New Testament teachings call the believer to a greater degree of involvement than the Old Testament expectations.

The life and ministry of Jesus emphasizes this building on Old Testament pronouncements. In his first sermon `following the wilderness temptations Jesus selects as his text Isaiah 61:1-2.

> The Spirit of the Lord is upon Me,
> Because He anointed Me to preach the gospel to the poor.
> He has sent Me to proclaim release to the captives,
> And recovery of sight to the blind,
> To set free those who are downtrodden,
> To proclaim the favorable year of the Lord (Luke 2:18-19).

To the persons gathered in the synagogue Jesus declares that the Scripture he has read is descriptive of his life and ministry (Luke 4:21). His ministry will be one that makes a vital difference in the lives of people who are poor and needy. The kingdom he inaugurates will care for those who hunger.

Even the joyous song of Mary picks up the theme of God's compassion for the poor and the standard of the new covenant. She speaks, "He has filled the hungry with good things; and sent away the rich empty-handed" (Luke 1:53).

In his teachings Jesus reiterates the increased expectations of the new covenant. In the Sermon on the Mount, Jesus quotes the regulations of the old covenant, then applies his interpretation that is far more demanding. In his "you have heard it said of old but I say unto you . . ." Jesus makes explicit the increased expectations of the process of grace as opposed to the old system of law.

The demands of genuine discipleship are illustrated by the fact that the disciples "left everything and followed Him" (Luke 5:11). In a discussion with his disciples Jesus speaks of the economic reorientation that is a part of the new covenant.

> And He said to his disciples, "For this reason I say to you, do not be anxious for your life, as to what you shall eat; nor for your body, as to what you shall put on. For life is more than food, and the body than clothing. Consider the ravens, for they neither sow nor reap; and they have no storeroom nor barn; and yet God feeds them; how much more valuable you are than the birds! And which of you by being anxious can add a single cubit to his life's span? If then you cannot do even a very little thing, why are you anxious about other matters? Consider the lilies, how they grow; they neither toil nor spin; but I tell you, even Solomon in all his glory did not clothe himself like one of these. But if God so arrays the grass in the field, which is alive today and tomorrow is thrown into the furnace, how much more will He clothe you, O men of little faith! And do not seek what you shall eat, and what you shall drink, and do not keep worrying. For all these things the nations of the world eagerly seek; but your Father knows that you need these things. But seek for His kingdom, and these things shall be added to you. Do not be afraid, little flock, for your Father has chosen gladly to give you the kingdom. Sell your possessions and give to charity; make yourselves purses which do not wear out, an unfailing treasure in heaven, where no thief comes near, nor moth destroys. For where your treasure is, there will your heart be also" (Luke 12:22-34).

In another passage Luke records Jesus' instruction to count the cost of the new covenant before making an allegiance to it.

For which one of you, when he wants to build a tower, does not first sit down and calculate the cost, to see if he has enough to complete it? Otherwise, when he has laid a foundation, and is not able to finish, all who observe it begin to ridicule him, saying, 'This man began to build and was not able to finish.' Or what king, when he sets out to meet another king in battle, will not first sit down and take counsel whether he is strong enough with ten thousand men to encounter the one coming against him with twenty thousand? Or else, while the other is still far away, he sends a delegation and asks terms of peace. So therefore, no one of you can be My disciple who does not give up all his own possessions. Therefore, salt is good; but if even salt has become tasteless, with what will it be seasoned? It is useless either for the soil or for the manure pile; it is thrown out. He who has ears to hear, let him hear" (Luke 14:28-35).

The new covenant calls believers to restructure their lives in such a way that reflects the priority of the kingdom of God. Such a reordering of priorities has powerful implications for ministry to the hungry. As Christians are freed from the materialistic quest, they are enabled to use their resources to benefit the lives of the poor and hungry.

As contemporary Christians face the world hunger crisis, it is important to heed the admonition of James 2:15-16. "If a brother or sister is without clothing and in need of daily food, and one of you says to them, 'Go in peace, be warmed and be filled'; and yet you do not give them what is necessary for their body; what use is that?" Responsible Christian response to the hunger crisis is more than awareness of the devastating need and the offering of gracious expressions of concern; it is action that alleviates need.

Such practical action on the behalf of the poor and hungry is natural for those who have experienced the love of God. Our actions in response to those in need give evidence to the reality of the love of God in us. First John 3:17-18 summarizes our Christian responsibility. "But whoever has the world's goods, and beholds his brother in need and closes his heart against him, how does the love of God abide in him? Little children, let us not love with word or with tongue, but in deed and truth."

Because the Christian lives by the new covenant rather than by the requirements of the old covenant, he is freed to respond to human need around him not out of obligation created by the law but out of gratitude produced by grace. The expectations for the righteous are greater in the new covenant, but the motivation for responsible Christian living is also greater. We live by love rather than law.

For Thought and Discussion

1. What kind of attitude does the Bible reveal on the part of God toward poor and hungry people? What Old Testament passages underscore his attitude? What does his attitude imply for us?

2. Is food a basic human right? Why or why not? What biblical passages support your conclusions?

3. Does any relationship exist between the biblical doctrine of sin and the problem of world hunger? If so, how does it relate? What biblical evidences do you have for your answer?

4. What did Jesus mean when he said, "The poor you have with you always"? Who is responsible for meeting the needs of hungry people? Which passages in the Bible give us instructions at this point? Discuss them.

5. According to the Bible what are Christians' responsibilities concerning people who are poor and hungry? How can we begin to follow the Bible's teaching?

3
What Does Theology Have to Do with Bloated Bellies?

What one believes about God makes a difference in the way he behaves toward other people. Theology has a place in a book about hunger.

This look at theology will be brief. Certain beliefs, however, are particularly relevant to meeting human need. Some theological concepts have been slighted, almost ignored. Other ideas about God have been distorted until they are of no earthly use. Christians facing world hunger need a working theology.

The Nature of God

One of the Christian notions about God with special meaning for anyone concerned about endangered human life is the idea that God is Creator of the universe. To begin at the beginning, it all comes from him (Gen. 1:1).

If one really believes that God made it all and keeps the world going (Acts 17:28), then the believer is simply a caretaker, not the owner of the natural resources about him. Men are trustees, managers of the limited land, air, and water.

The Christian sees God as the one who gives all good things (Jas. 1:17) and expects the recipient to make good use of them (Luke 12:48). From the first, man was instructed to "replenish the earth, and subdue it: and have dominion over . . . every living thing" (Gen. 1:28). The first man was put in the Garden of Eden "to dress it and to keep it" (Gen. 2:15).

Today that replenishing, subduing, and having dominion

might clearly involve the development of solar energy, the exploration of the oceans as food sources, and the extension of productive agriculture to unused lands. Dressing and keeping the earth-gift demands recognition of its finiteness. Acceptance of the limitedness of fossil fuels, for instance, invokes a good stewardship of them.

Believing that God created the heavens and the earth implies that man is to be a careful manager of the gifts God has loaned him for a lifetime. How ironic, then, that some would defend emotionally their doctrine of God as Creator in a pulpit harangue delivered in a wastefully air-conditioned auditorium to an overstuffed people who will drive their gas-guzzling cars to a restaurant for big, juicy steaks after the sermon. If, indeed, God *is* Creator, that truth has implications for the way his people handle his gift. They ask, Am I supporting famine by the way I live?

Closely related to this doctrine is the idea that God alone is worthy of worship (Ex. 20:3). The first of the Ten Commandments prohibits the worship of any other deity but Jehovah. It establishes the Creator God as the one valid object of worship, awe, and adoration.

It is not stretching the point to say that for all practical purposes many persons today worship success or the "good life." There is an idolatry of narrow nationalism (America, love it or leave it) and a form of materialism (does it pay?) that takes the place of God.

There are more subtle forms of idolatry. Some of those studying world hunger have reduced the problems to economic projections. The over reliance on the study of economics (economism) is no less idolatry than the implicit belief that science has all the answers (scientism). Then there are others still trapped in the simplified belief in inevitable progress. They say that growth is good, and bigger is better, and they expect the world's problems to be solved by the sheer dent of human effort.

One idolatry is as bad as another. They all ignore the God worthy of this sort of single-minded devotion.

Another belief particularly relevant to meeting human need is the Christian understanding of the nature of God. If God is and is the one worshiped, the sort of God he is does matter.

What is there about God that helps us know how to respond to hungry people? God is a moral person, not an abstract principle. He is just and righteous and holy. He is "light" (1 John 1:5) and "love" (1John 4:8). He is the sovereign God of the universe, yet he is the caring Father. All of these characteristics of God challenge believers to be like him and reveal his attitude toward those in need of him.

Further, the idea that man is made in the image of God (Gen. 1:27) is a concept of such importance that any difference between one person and another is relatively insignificant. Not enough has been made of the belief that all persons individually are created like God and capable of responding to him (Ps. 8).

Julius K. Nyerere, President of Tanzania, says: "We say man was created in the image of God. I refuse to imagine a God who is miserable, poor, ignorant, superstitious, fearful, oppressed and wretched–which is the lot of the majority of those He created in His own image."[1]

This teaching that man is made in God's image invests in individuals a worth and dignity that allows no easy escape from ethical responsibility. After all, each one is a replica of God himself.

International policies should not deny lightly aid to starving peoples. Western nations cannot justify as Christian a sort of passive genocide, such as triage, that conspires to refuse help to some of the hungry with slim chances of survival.

Norman Cousins says it well.

Desensitization, not hunger, is the greatest curse on earth. It begins by calibrating people's credentials to live and ends by cheapening all life.

Famine in India and Bangladesh is a test not just of our capacity to respond as human beings, but of our ability to understand the cycles of civilization. We can't ignore out-stretched hands without destroying that which is most significant in the American character—a sense of vital identification with human beings wherever they are. Regarding life as the highest value is more important to the future of America than anything we make or sell.[2]

Kin to the Christian understanding of persons as made in God's image is belief in the oneness of the human family. This belief in the solidarity of the human race has been slighted. It is a prominent theme in the Scriptures.

John Donne's "No man is an island . . . any man's death diminishes me, because I am involved in mankind" sounds very much like Saint Paul's "none of us liveth to himself, and no man dieth to himself" (Rom. 14:7).

Some opponents of massive aid to famine-hit countries such as Garrett Hardin of the University of California use the analogy of the lifeboat. They say that if the survivors permit more than a certain number on board, everyone will go down. Most Christian sympathies would more likely be with the late G. K. Chesterton, who said, "We are all in a small boat in a stormy sea and we owe each other a terrible loyalty." Both our value and our oneness or solidarity are derived from the very nature of God.

Can you imagine a follower of Jesus Christ praying, "Give *me* this day *my* daily bread"? The nature of sin is close to that sort of self-centeredness.

There are corporate and national implications for this belief in the solidarity of the human family under God. If Christians worship and serve the God of all mankind, then they are more interested in working with others than in going it alone. Christians are more committed to cooperation with other peoples than competition with them.

This shrinking planet is too small, its resources too limited, time for change is too short for Christians to follow the political rhetoric of those who would set our nation against the rest of the world. Cooperation is the only sensible way to approach the energy crisis and other shortages. Besides that, it is the Christian way.

The Mission of Christ

The way God revealed himself in Jesus Christ lifts the value of the individual to an even higher level. The coming of Jesus Christ, his death and resurrection have meaning for the struggle with hunger.

The Christian belief that God was uniquely in the person of Jesus Christ is known as the doctrine of the incarnation. The Gospel reports it in simple words. "The Word was made flesh, and dwelt among us" (John 1:14).

This understanding of a God who elevated human flesh by taking it upon himself is radical in its implications for the worth of persons. God is no longer seen as "out there" somewhere by those who accept his incarnation, in-fleshment in Jesus Christ.

God showed us in Christ that he was willing to play the game by rules he had made. He demonstrated that he was willing to take his own medicine. He voluntarily chose to identify with humankind as fully as possible (Phil. 2:5-10).

The Christian understanding of a God who became fully human speaks clearly for a working theology to combat hunger. First, an incarnational theology takes seriously all human concerns, suffering, aches, pains, and problems. Nothing human is alien to the believer who remembers that Jesus Christ himself wore a body like ours with all its limitations. In getting tired, having ingrown toenails, going hungry, being tempted, cutting his thumb, he dignified and valued all human flesh as it had never before been elevated.

The most remote, hungry little child has significance, worth, importance that she could not possess apart from God's high estimate of human worth evidenced in Jesus Christ. God, by investing deity in a human body, put the price of one person's physical life above anything other religions or systems can approach. Archbishop William Temple was right in suggesting that in this way, at least, Christianity is the most materialistic of the world's religions. Christians take the stuff of life seriously. Followers of Jesus surely take seriously the hurt, agony, starvation, and death of hungry people.

Beyond that, believers cannot escape the demands for involvement made by the incarnaton. Withdrawal is impossible. The tough problems, controversies, and conflicts of life are the natural habitat for followers of Jesus. Since the incarnation is the ultimate involvement, no escape to a pietistic, "spiritual" religion is possible for those who follow Christ.

A certain brand of religion has gloried in retreat from the harsh realities of physical existence. Some worshipers take their gospel songs literally and would like to live on a mountain "underneath a cloudless sky" or reach the point where "the things of earth will grow strangely dim in the light of His glory and grace."

The Jesus who took upon himself the sufferings of those about him was no "cop-out Christ." His commitment to mankind was total. His involvement was complete. To the degree that those who claim his name follow him, they will in-flesh their theology. Helping hungry people is a necessary corollary of any incarnational theology in today's situation.

Beyond the incarnation the life and teachings of Jesus are an important element in a functional theology for facing world hunger. (See chapter 2.) Jesus, by his words and deeds, set a pattern of caring for hurting humankind. What he did and said about the poor, the hungry, the naked, the prisoner has been too largely ignored, spiritualized, and dismissed as inapplicable to the current hunger problem. Curiously, some who contend that the Bible should be taken literally are the first to insist that Jesus' concern was for "spiritual" hunger, "spiritual" thirst, and "spiritual" poverty. That is convenient. It does not cost anything.

The crucifixion of Jesus has continuing meaning for followers of the Christ. It was a historical event on an actual hill at a specific point in time. Yet all of Christendom has seen the abiding relevance of the cross. The way to God for one today, as always, involves acceptance of the redemptive work done on the cross by Jesus Christ.

The cross has a place in a practical theology for facing problems like world hunger. It is "the unifying symbol of a distinctly Christian life" as T. B. Maston says. The cross is more than that. The cross reveals fully God's love for man and his hatred for sin. Man could never have known fully either of these had Christ not died on the cross. Disciples of Christ do have these parallel insights. So crossbearers do not make lame excuses about their lack of compassion for those haunting, hungry faces. The very cross in which followers of Christ claim redemption is the seal of God's love for all mankind, even those with bloated bellies and bony faces. The ones who kneel at the cross have no difficulty mustering and sustaining indignation and anger at the power of corporate evil. They have seen evil at its worst. The very selfishness and greed that killed Christ is at work in the world today killing other innocents.

The cross-life means that those who follow him will, like him, seek not their own will but the will of God (John 20:21). It means a giving of self and a sacrifice of privilege. It means changing society by the power of love, self-denial, putting others first, and voluntary surrender of self with a redemptive, uplifting purpose.

The meaning of the cross for contemporary life has been terribly narrowed, distorted, and perverted by those who see it only as the symbol of personal salvation. The cross makes us care about one another and ends hostility (Eph. 2:16). The cross is central in a Christian social strategy. As T. B. Maston says: "This involves the returning of good for evil, the strong serving the weak, the privileged taking the initiative in working out the problems of the underprivileged, even the just to a degree taking upon themselves the sins of the unjust."[3]

Even the New Testament doctrine of the resurrection has something to do with a theology for facing world hunger. The Christian belief that Jesus Christ actually did rise from the grave and literally conquer death is a source of real hope. Jesus said, "Because I live, ye shall live also" (John 14:19).

This belief is far more than simply a personal promise of immortality. For believers there is a different look toward the future than for those who do not have the promise that comes with the resurrection.

God is in history. He is not through with man. He is still in control. All of this means that efforts for change are never wasted. A passive resignation to the evils of the day is sinful. The one who knows to do good and does not do it is guilty of real sin (Jas. 4:17).

Christians have some sense of responsibility for the future. It is easy to understand the difficulty of mustering sufficient motivation to make the needed changes if the world is to avoid starvation and ecological calamity.

Robert L. Heilbroner puts it well in a chapter entitled "What Has Posterity Ever Done for Me?"

> Will Mankind survive? Who knows? The question I want to put is more searching: Who cares? It is clear that most of us today do not care–or at least do not care enough. How many of us would be willing to give up some minor convenience–say, the use of aerosols–in

the hope that this might extend the life of man on earth by a hundred years? Suppose we also know with a high degree of certainty that humankind could not survive a thousand years unless we gave up our wasteful diet of meat, abandoned all pleasure driving, cut back on every use of energy that was not essential to the maintenance of a bare minimum. Would we care enough for posterity to pay the price of its survival? . . . Even a century far exceeds our powers of empathetic imagination.[4]

Yet believers in Jesus Christ have the quality of hope for the future that permits, no, demands that they work at identifying with those yet unborn. The Christian has a theology of hope. God is out ahead of us beckoning us on. God is not trapped in history, a thing of the past or up there somewhere out of touch with reality. Neither is the living God simply within us, confined to our apathy.

God is, rather, leading us, going before us as he led the children of Israel in the exodus from Egypt. He is in and behind and under and above all the events of the week ahead, the years ahead, waiting for us to catch up.

An eschatology (study of last things) that is genuinely Christian is not so concerned with signs of the end times as with sharing the blessed hope that is held in Jesus Christ. Precisely that ingredient, hope, is the one thing most necessary for tackling the problems related to world hunger.

An intelligent base of ideas is essential for confronting any difficult social problem. A logically consistent system of thought is necessary for dealing with complex, mind-boggling issues like world hunger. A world view that hangs together, linked with a magnificent obsession which commands more than simply rational interest, must be found for fighting hunger.

Allegiance to Jesus Christ claims heart and mind and soul and strength. Christian theology offers some hope as the base of operations for fighting hunger.

For Thought and Discussion

1. Discuss the doctrine of man's creation in the image of God. What does that imply for the world hunger crisis? What other implications may be drawn from the belief?

2. What do you understand the following terms to mean?

   scientism
   economism
   idolatry
   genocide
   incarnation

3. Does the cross of Jesus Christ have any meaning for social, political, and economic questions? What are those implications as they relate to world hunger?

4. Why should Christians care about the future? Is the Christian motivation for dealing with the future any different from that of the nonbeliever? If so, how?

4
What Would Move Me to Help Hungry People?

Good persons are willing to respond to world hunger needs. The decent fellow who is personally moral as a Christian is ready to relate to the food crisis. Christian ethics has social as well as personal dimensions. One cannot choose between personal ethics and social concern. If either is genuine, the other is implied.

The logical extension of individual morality is a social ethic. Christian love is not limited to those whom we can touch with our hands. The universality of the gospel message includes its moral implications just as it applies to its redemptive purpose. There is nothing provincial or parochial about Christian ethics.

The deeper one's individual concern for persons, the more effectively he wants to see love buttressed by law. The more authentic one's personal morality, the more extensively he wants to see Christians engaged in social action. It is the same love for persons—made in God's image, bought with the blood of Jesus Christ—that motivates personal morality and social concern. The more intense his compassion for one hungry person, the more genuine his interest in global justice.

The mature Christian ethic is marked by concern for the physical as well as the spiritual dimensions of life. Followers of Jesus are interested in bodies as well as souls.

Martin Luther King, Jr., spoke to this theme.

> The gospel at its best deals with the whole man . . . not only his spiritual well-being but also his material well-being. A religion that

"For I was hungry..."

> professes a concern for the souls of men and is not equally concerned about the slums that damn them, the economic conditions that strangle them, and the social conditions that cripple them, is a spiritually moribund religion.[1]

The churchmember who supports foreign mission work, believes in evangelism, and rejoices in revival is said to "love souls." While one can understand the figure of speech, let us hope that he loves persons, not just souls. Over half the world's souls will go to bed without enough to eat tonight. Christians care about bodies, too.

When the popular American cowboy Gene Autry had a radio program, he sang a so-called gospel song that captured the sentiment of many churchgoers. The first line said, "There's a gold mine in the sky some sweet day." That sums up the Christian faith for many.

The Harvard theologian Amos N. Wilder comments on otherworldly religion.

> Many of our contemporaries are inclined to say that the Christian conviction of things not seen and the Resurrection hope mean escapism, pie-in-the-sky, the opium of the people, what they call "compensatory fictions." . . . The man in the street is shrewdly aware of these deformations in much Christianity as taught and practiced. One could make a list of the often merciless . . . plaster-of-Paris saints, Holy Joes, swooning mystics, cataleptic revivalists, jaundiced Sabbatarians, professional do-gooders, weeping Jeremiahs, anemic Galahads, religious masochists, etc.[2]

Authentic Christianity, however, is concerned with the here-and-now as well as with the by-and-by. Paul refers to believers as "having promise of the life that now is, and of that which is to come" (1 Tim. 4:8). Churchmen are ready to grapple with the hunger issue because their faith is applicable to the moment. It works today.

A Faith That Works

That is the next point. The Christian religion is built on a faith that works. There is an action-ethic aspect to all Christianity worthy of the name.

What doth it profit, my brethren, though a man say he hath faith, and have not works? can faith save him? If a brother or sister be naked, and destitute of daily food, and one of you say unto them, Depart in peace, be ye warmed and filled; notwithstanding ye give them not those things which are needful to the body; what doth it profit? Even so faith, if it hath not works, is dead, being alone" (Jas. 2:14-17).

The religious and ethical sides of Christianity are really inseparable. Like the Jews before them, the early Christians did not make neat distinctions between the vertical and horizontal relationships.

Vital Christianity today responds to those who are naked and destitute of daily food. A draggy, lazy, apathetic faith is inexcusable. For faith to fail or to delay its action actually extends human suffering.

Christians understand that intertwining as it was described by Dietrich Bonhoeffer. "If the hungry man does not attain to faith, then the guilt falls on those who refused him bread. To provide the hungry man with bread is to prepare the way for the coming of grace."[3]

Sloth in service, intellectualized theology, empty pietism, emotional fits of religious fervor, obsession with the study of last things, and preoccupation with the doctrine of the Holy Spirit or some other important but single New Testament doctrine, all describe Christianity as it is actually practiced in many churches. All of the above flunk the test of the kind of faith described in the New Testament. A biblical faith works. Faith is doing the will of God. That truth offers hope to hungry people.

A Love That Really Cares

In real life it is a phony distinction to separate faith and love. In the New Testament they go together. "Faith which worketh by love" (Gal. 5:6). Georgia Harkness offers an analysis of the relationship. "It appears that *pistis* (faith) is very intimately connected with love and it is 'faith working through love' that sums up the Christian's moral obligation."[4]

This overarching obligation is somewhat paradoxical in nature. It is an obligation that is fulfilled in love. Not dry duty or awful oughtness, it is the love that Jesus called the greatest commandment (Mark 12:29-30).

This love spoken of is the test for Christian ethics. It is the central ethical principle. Without love, no action, not even the most severe self-sacrifice, is completely ethical in quality (1 Cor. 13:3).

The love required by the New Testament is a tough kind of love. Mere sentiment will not satisfy God or help feed hungry children. It is a love that goes on loving when it does not get loved back. It is a love that loves persons whom one has never met. It is a love that is in no way dependent upon reciprocity (Matt. 5:43-46).

That sounds simple enough. Love others and be right with God. It is not so easy. Who can say that he measures up perfectly?

Yet there is a very practical, common sense measure of love. Martin Luther described it.

> If you want to know how you ought to love your neighbor, ask yourself how much you love yourself. If you were to get into trouble or danger, you would be glad to have the love and help of all men. You do not need any book of instructions to teach you how to love your neighbor.[5]

Somehow this love ethic must be activated to overcome the indifference that plagues Christians facing world hunger. Morally does it matter whether a man is killed in a war or is condemned to die of starvation by apathy?

A dying child evokes a unique response when one holds him in his arms as the child dies. A nun who works in a children's hospital in Calcutta says, "They die so gracefully." Yet the death of thousands becomes a boring statistic. We hear that thousands die, and we yawn in response.

It is possible that only the unique love ethic of Christianity can provide the motive power needed to change personal life-styles. The ideal, the goal of loving neighbor as one's self, is directly related to the problem of hunger. For instance, a small portion of the world's people are over eating (a euphemism for gluttony) while most persons on the earth today literally do not have enough for minimal health standards.

In the Old Testament there are a lot of passages about rights and wrongs concerning eating. Love for others is the determining factor in several New Testament passages that relate to eating habits (Rom. 14:15; 1 Cor. 6:13; 8:13). Whatever else the Christian ethic teaches about love, it is clear that love behaves just the opposite from greedy, grasping self service. We will not choke or guzzle or waste our way to blessedness.

Wealth is often the evidence of greed and an unloving heart. The hoarding of vast riches and accumulation of unneeded luxury will not mix with Christian service. "No one can serve two masters. . . . Ye cannot serve God and mammon" (Matt. 6:24; Luke 16:13). "It is easier for a camel to go through the eye of a needle, than for a rich man to enter the kingdom of God" (Mark 10:25).

Yet it is amazing to observe how Christian institutions and individuals have rationalized, justified and even honored acquiring possessions. The biblical sin of avarice has been glorified as an evidence of personal industry and thriftiness. The holding of unused wealth, the building of seldom used church buildings and the investing in unnecessary luxury is practiced by many churches and condoned in churchmembers.

Is it possible that Christian love may hold greed in check? Nothing less than changed lives and loving persons will conquer greed.

A Freedom That Is Shared

A faith that works and a love that cares are also related to basic Christian freedom. It is freedom for which we are set free according to Galatians 5:1.

Christians who care about hungry persons recognize with Adlai E. Stevenson that "a hungry man is not a free man." Personal freedom is essential for the realization of one's full humanity. A Christian ethic that slights that truth is incomplete. There can be no justice or dignity when there is not free choice and freely chosen action for the welfare of others. R. H. Tawney in the classic *Religion and the Rise of Capitalism* wrote: "Since even quite common men have souls, no increase in material wealth will compensate them for arrangements which insult their self-respect and impair their freedom."

Freedom, then, is one major objective in any Christian ethic for confronting hunger. The freedom of the hungry persons as well as the freedom of the helping persons should always be kept in mind. Christians will not force their ethical codes upon those to whom they minister.

On the other hand, Christian liberty does not release believers from the bonds of love. Luther corrected those who took their Christian freedom as an excuse to evade responsibility. Some Christ-claimers have always said, "If salvation is not a matter of works, why should we do anything for the hungry?" Luther answered those false ideas.

> In this crude manner they turn the liberty of the spirit into wantonness and licentiousness. We want them to know, however, that if they use

their lives and possessions after their own pleasure, if they do not help the poor, if they cheat their fellow-men in business and snatch and scrape by hook and by crook everything they can lay their hands on, we want to tell them that they are not free, no matter how much they think they are, but they are the dirty slaves of the devil, and are seven times worse than they ever were as the slaves of the Pope.[6]

Freedom, then, offers a motive for helping hungry people. No one can realize liberty if he is struggling to survive. Freedom is also a necessary condition for those who would voluntarily and willingly extend food and life and help to those who are starving. Christians deliberately choose to give themselves. It is for freedom that they are set free.

A Justice That Is More Than Order

The Christian ethic is marked by the pursuit of justice. Justice in its simplest sense demands action on the hunger issue. More will be expected of the one to whom much has been given. More will be asked of him because he was entrusted with more (Luke 12:48). It is an elementary matter of justice.

Beyond this sort of mathematical fairness the New Testament appeal for a more profound justice is clear. Christian teaching does not allow evasion. As Barbara Ward puts it:

> Dives leaving Lazarus to sicken at his gate, the rich man rebuilding his barns for the selfish consumption of a larger harvest, the priest and levite 'passing by on the other side'—these parables of justice and judgment meet us on every page of the Bible and the final gathering in of God's people turns on one thing only—that the hungry are fed, the naked clothed, prisoners visited, the afflicted given comfort. These are gestures of love. But they are not left to our choice. Justice is the command to which love responds. To refuse is to 'choose death.'[7]

In a sinful, imperfect world, justice is often all that is possible when love is the goal. Many times one must settle for justice with the full knowledge that less than the biblical goal of love for one's neighbor has been attained. A certain rightness and straightness is expected by Christians as at least a rough approximation of the higher justice that they know is God's. The hymn writer spoke of this higher plane of justice.

There's a wideness in God's mercy,
Like the wideness of the sea;
There's a kindness in His justice,
Which is more than liberty.

The Christian struggle for justice, then, is not unrelated to the freedom that is known in Christ. That freedom, as seen above, is inextricably linked to a working faith and the morality that has love as its central principle.

A Cross That Offers the Christian Distinctive

The place of the cross of Jesus Christ in a Christian ethic for today is more than a mere example or symbol of a principle. A "cross ethic" means a practiced theology of redemption. It means actually following a religion that requires sacrifice. It means deliberately being set apart, different, "peculiar" if necessary because Jesus Christ was so set apart on the cross.

Following an ethic of the cross involves self-giving of a more radical sort than token charity calls for. It literally involves being a person for others. Can a person living today possibly identify himself as a follower of one who died on a cross for mankind without some of the same self-giving? The screamed recommendations of the cross as the only way to God often are made meaningless by the very lives of the screamers. This is true if cross-preachers show no understanding that persons are now dying because the cross-life is not evident among believers. We who wear the cross in our lapels have to consume less energy, own fewer goods, waste less food, and simplify our lives so that others may live. Until that is done, it is difficult for anyone to see how the cross has any relationship to Christian living. The cross-life may offer what is, after all, a higher standard of living.

A Principle That Unifies Christian Ethics

One could be confused looking at the various incentives for Christian living. Appeals to do the right thing about helping the hungry are based on all sorts of grounds. The Christian ethic is not a hodgepodge of random rules and disjointed duties. Christian moral conduct is not a patchwork quilt of unrelated moralisms. There is an unchanging center for the Christian life—"Jesus Christ the same yesterday, and to day, and for ever" (Heb. 13:8).

A living relationship with the living Lord makes Christian ethics dynamic and comprehensive. The believer is concerned with doing God's will. God cares about all persons and all the world. Hence, by seeking to do God's will above all else, the Christian ethic offers a systems approach to fighting world hunger.

Do we need to recognize the inevitable consequences of misusing the limited resources of the earth and violating the basic laws of the universe? Written into those laws is the truth "whatsoever a man soweth, that shall he also reap" (Gal. 6:7). The industrial West used "cheap" oil to speed its development. Next we were hooked on oil. Now we are paying the consequences for the habit.

Do we need a new world consciousness to release us from narrow nationalism? Christians have it if they will be true to their understanding of all persons being made in God's image and the related oneness of the human family.

Do we need a new attitude based on harmony and cooperation rather than conflict and competition? The message of Jesus that makes love central offers that attitude (Matt. 5).

Do we need a balance between personal freedom and social responsibility? The ethic outlined in Paul's writings speaks precisely to that problem (Gal. 5).

Do we need some signs of hope for mankind? The identification with the future that is a part of Christian doctrine offers a new attitude, a new assurance with respect to the course of social events.

Do we need something to pull together the positive elements of a Christian ethic for combatting world hunger? A genuine, personal commitment to doing the will of God offers the integrating force needed. The ideal and the incentive are one. The highest good is at the same time the way to achieve that goal. The love of God, continually demonstrating that his will is best for men, is subjectively appropriated without losing its objective character.

To do the will of God personally and corporately *is* the ethical approach. God wants the best for humankind.

For Thought and Discussion

1. What is the relationship between personal morality and social ethics? How does that relationship affect world hunger?
2. How does Christian love relate to the basic Christian ethic? Why is love thought to be so important? Give your own definition or characterization of *agape*. See 1 Corinthians 13:1-8 in J. B. Phillips translation of the New Testament, *The New Testament in Modern English.*
3. See if you can find some of the many Old Testament passages related to dietary laws. Is there a modern, common sense application of these passages?
4. Discuss the nature and limitations of Christian freedom. What does the limitation of freedom have to do with world hunger?

5
Who Emptied the Cupboard?

The battle is often intense: hunger versus the will to live. People do not easily let go of life. Throughout the Fourth World, the battle is acted out in slow-motion cameos of desperation: a father wandering the streets hunting work, any work; a mother who has no milk clinging to her dying baby; a little girl who no longer has strength to fight on the streets for food; an old woman with the appearance of a skeleton painted brown who waits and prays for death.

For many like these, hunger already has triumphed over the will to live. In recent years hundreds of thousands have died in Bangladesh. No one knows how many have died in the Sahel, that arid part of West Africa that lies between the Sahara on the north and the tropical rain forests on the south. In India, official reluctance to admit the extent of poverty fails to conceal the fact that millions have died.

How Bad Is It?

A vast portion of mankind is looking in the cupboard and finding it bare. The enormity of the problem is hard to grasp. More than a billion people are malnourished, lacking enough calories or protein to lead a normal life. Another five hundred million people are in the process of starving to death.

For ten million people a year the cupboard has been bare too long. They will die from starvation or hunger-related diseases.

One of every five deaths in the world is from hunger. Every minute of every day starvation triumphs over the struggle to survive in twenty lives. For many others, survival is balanced precariously on the edge of this year's harvest.

Geographically most starvation is in forty-eight countries that frequently are referred to as the *Fourth World*. The Fourth World consists of those countries that are the world's worst economic hardship cases. *Third World* refers to developing countries, many of which are still very poor. *Second World* refers to Communist states and *First World* to the other developed industrial countries. *Most Seriously Affected* countries (MSA's) are those that have been designated by the United Nations as hardest hit by adverse global, agricultural, and economic conditions. In 1974, there were thirty-three countries designated as MSA's. The number is now well over forty and continues to increase.[1]

The Fourth World stretches like a belt worn just below the fat waist of the world. Most Fourth World countries are found in Africa, the Middle East and Southeast Asia. Typical of these are Upper Volta, Ethiopia, India, Bangladesh, and Honduras.

Starvation is personal, however, not merely geographical. Hunger happens to people. True, the results frequently are manifested in social upheaval and political turmoil, but these are symptoms of the disease of desperation.

The dictionary definition sheds little light on what hunger really is. *Hunger:* "the weakness, debilitation, or pain caused by a prolonged lack of food; starvation." It is not the dictionary's fault. There are no words that describe adequately the continual day and night craving for food or the slow wasting away of flesh as the body consumes itself because it has nothing else to eat.

There are, of course, words that attempt to describe what hunger does to the human body. The academic terms do little more than provide insulation from the horrible realities.

Kwashiorkor: "severe malnutrition characterized by anemia, edema, pot-belly. . . ." Kwashiorkor is bloated bodies and dull eyes reflecting the suffering and brain damage that are its companions.

Marasmus: "A wasting away of the body, associated with inadequate or inadequately assimilated food." The reality is wrinkled skin drawn tightly over bones, stick figures with bloated bellies, children with old people's faces, diarrhea, dehydration, a ravenous craving for food.

The words almost become a barrier to understanding the incomprehensible human suffering. The reality can be evaded for only so long, however, as the specter of starvation looms at the edge of billions of human lives.

How has it happened? What are the ingredients that have led to the present human catastrophe, the ramifications of which none of mankind will escape?

The Economic Gap

The basic ingredient is money or the lack of it. Hunger is a result of poverty. There is currently enough food produced in the world to feed everyone adequately. If a person has money, that person can buy food. The problem is distribution. While some folks in the world are consuming so much their health is threatened, others are eating so little their lives are threatened. Gandhi said, "There is enough for every man's need but not enough for every man's greed."

The economic gap between the rich and poor people of the world is enormous. Those who have gotten most of the international pie are continually getting more of it. It has not always been so. At the beginning of the nineteenth century the difference in per capita income between the poor and rich nations was one to two. The ratio now stands at one to twenty and continues to widen.[2] In the less developed countries the per capita gross national product is $275, while in the developed countries it is $4,050.[3] The poor literally are getting poorer. World Bank President Robert McNamara has noted that the per capita income of the one billion people living in the poorest countries declined an average .5 percent in 1974 and that another decrease is likely for 1975.[4]

The "eternal compulsory fast" that Mahatma Gandhi described continues. Mahbub ul Haq has described the economic gap: "When you rip aside the confusing figures on growth rates, you find that for about two-thirds of humanity the increase in per capita income has been less than one dollar a year for the last 20 years." [5]

There is little doubt that the gap will continue to widen. The international systems of trade and finance are controlled by the haves, not the have-nots. Tariffs, interest rates, monopolies, insurance rates, transportation, and other components of international finance are controlled almost entirely by the developed countries.

Essentially, this means that the fate of the underdeveloped world rests in the hands of developed nations. Although the underdeveloping world increases its demand for international justice, it has little power. The decisions that will lead to justice for the most part will be made in the developed world. Before any fundamental changes in the systems can be made, the haves must determine whether to take all they can from the have-nots. Former President Lyndon B. Johnson in his last public speech warned, "An island of plenty cannot exist for long in a world of want."

That underdeveloped countries are dissatisfied with their fate resting in the hands of others is understandable. In many instances their poverty is due largely to treatment they have received from the developed world. The plunder mentality of colonizing countries such as France, England, Spain, Holland, and Portugal resulted in a massive loss of precious resources in many underdeveloped countries. And even though political subservience for the most part has ended, economic submission has continued with effects that are just as devastating.

Nor have recent developments been encouraging for the poorer nations. In particular, the growing scarcity of two products on the international market, food and oil, has had a significant impact.

The increase in food prices came first. In the early 1970s, the major grain-producing countries (principally the United States) discovered that world food demand was coming very close to outstripping supply. This was caused partially from unusually low production in some countries and partially from the decisions of Russia and Japan to expand livestock herds. Increased herds meant the need for increased feed, so the Soviets purchased massive amounts of grain in 1972.

The United States realized that food could be priced about as high as the producer chose to go without significantly reducing demand. Food is an essential commodity. Those who need it have no choice but to buy, no matter what the price.

In 1972, the United States earned $7 billion from commercial farm exports. By 1974, that figure had risen to over $20 billion. Earnings from poor countries jumped from $1.6 billion to $6.6 billion during that time.[6] From 1973 to 1974, the food bill paid by the underdeveloped countries went from $3 billion to $6 billion. The burden, of course, fell most heavily on those countries that had the smallest capital reserve. To buy food, many underdeveloped countries had to borrow heavily from capital sources in developed countries. The United States benefited not only from the increased profits for its food but also from the interest that had to be paid on money borrowed to buy our food.

The oil embargo, with its subsequent jump in oil prices, began in October, 1973, and continued for five months. This was the second major blow to the international economy. Poor countries which did not produce oil saw trade deficits skyrocket as they tried to purchase oil and oil-based products. Ironically, countries that were trying desperately to increase food production to avoid paying the higher food prices found themselves unable to do so. Items essential to increased food production, fuel and fertilizer, suddenly were priced out of reach.

The increases the Fourth World countries paid for oil, food, and fertilizer in the mid-1970s devoured most of their foreign exchange. From 1971 to 1974, the cost of ten million tons of grain increased from $850 million to $2,080 million; the cost of one million tons of manufactured fertilizer went from $116 million to $296 million; and the cost of oil imports went from $5 billion to $15-17 billion.[7]

The impact of the widening economic gap must not be understood in terms of dollars alone. The ultimate impact is seen in human lives as the governments of the less developed countries increasingly are unable to provide services, food, education, health care, and the necessary financial backing for long-term development projects. The economic gap is unjust. The expansion of that gap must be halted and the trend reversed before the majority of mankind has any hope for self-improvement.

Climate, Consumption, and Children

While the economic gap is the foundation on which much of the hunger problem is built, there are at least three other factors that have compounded the misery of millions: climate, consumption, and children.

While erratic weather is not the cause of lasting world hunger, it has made a major contribution to the crisis. Millions of people in rural areas live from crop to crop. Sometimes they are able to store enough reserves to allow partial failure of a crop. A total crop failure or successive failures leave them helpless.

Without money to purchase food, the only alternatives are to go to the city looking for work or to receive help from food relief programs. Too often, they find the cities already glutted and the relief programs inadequate. Without security in the countryside, a job in the city, or new land to farm, the rural victims of crop failure become "marginal people."

Thus changes in weather patterns have a life and death impact. Recently such changes have been all too frequent. In Africa's Sahel, the drought began about 1968. The rains became erratic, then stopped entirely. Crops failed and grazing lands dried up. Herdsmen cut brush for their cattle, further devastating the land.

For seven years the rains failed in the Sahel. Herds died as the Sahara steadily moved southward. For untold thousands who were never reached by international relief programs, the rains came too late.

In Northern India, the monsoons failed again in 1974. For the last decade every other year has been a drought year. Why the monsoons have been sporadic is unknown.

In Bangladesh, erratic weather brought disaster not from too little rain but from too much. The rains that failed in India fell on Bangladesh flooding two-thirds of the country. The effects on at least one family were graphically portrayed by Stanley Mooneyham.

> Jobeda, who sits in a refugee camp in Dacca waiting for death to take the sixth of her seven children, knows only that this time the waters washed away the last thread of her hope.
>
> Jobeda's husband was one of twenty-seven thousand deaths due to starvation reported as another result of the flood. It was too much for her. She pulled a few rags together, picked up a clay pot, gathered her remaining two children and went to Dacca in a last desperate effort to keep them alive. There she became a refugee statistic—one of twelve hundred in this camp—just as her husband and five of her children had become starvation statistics.
>
> When we saw her sitting stoically in the corner of a make-shift

hospital, she was emotionally wiped out. Jobeda had no tears left to cry. Lying at her feet, the two remaining children were too weak from malnutrition and sickness to do more than whimper.[8]

Whether these disasters of nature are due to fundamental climatic change is the source of much debate among scientists and meteorologists. What is known is that freakish weather has been more the rule than the exception in recent years and that the effects of these deviations have been disastrous for millions.

While part of the world starves, another part gorges. The uncontrolled consumption habits of much of the developed world must be considered another of the fundamental causes of world hunger. The appetites of the rich have become as much of a threat as the fertility of the poor.

Food consumption has increased to the point that it has become a health hazard. The average North American consumes a ton of grain a year, five times what the average person in the less developed countries consumes.[9] Americans out-eat citizens of India by more than five to one! [10]

Larger amounts of grain are being used in the developed world to fatten livestock, an extremely inefficient way to produce food. For every pound of beef produced, approximately ten pounds of grain will be used. Twenty-one pounds of grain protein are needed to produce one pound of beef protein.[11] It is true that some feed grain is not normally eaten by humans, but most of it could be used for human consumption. Rich nations currently feed their livestock more grain than the people of India and China, one-third of the human race, consume directly.[12]

This does not mean that beef production should be halted. It simply is not necessary to finish out beef with large amounts of grain. Grass-fed beef is as nourishing and has an important role in the food chain.

America's eating habits not only have international consequences; they have personal consequences. Americans consume more calories and three to four times more protein per day than is needed. Most Americans average an intake of 3,300 calories per day. Some experts have calculated that if the whole world ate like Americans and grew their food by American methods, the known world reserves of petroleum would be exhausted by agriculture alone within twenty-nine years.[13]

The United States uses 17.3 million barrels of petroleum a day, about 30 percent of the world's daily production. By contrast, all of Africa uses one million barrels a day and the Middle East consumes 1.5 million.[14]

With 6 percent of the world's population, North America consumes over 40 percent of the world's resources. One American consumes and pollutes as much as 50 or more African or Indian peasants.[15]

Nevertheless, all would be fine if this were a world of unlimited resources. It is not! If some have more, others have less. There is no way, for instance, that the whole world now could experience the standard of living of the developed world. There is not that much to go around. The repercussions of the American appetite are felt around the world. Less consumption in this country does not necessarily mean that the food, energy, or resources that are saved will be used elsewhere. That depends upon many economic and political factors. But less consumption at least creates the possibility of that which is saved being available to others. "There is no escaping the conclusion that at present rates of growth the world population will soon exceed our capacity to provide food and other necessary natural resources. Either the birth rate must come down or the death rate must go up."[16]

When will population overload be reached? No one knows for sure, of course, but it is becoming apparent that the torrent of human growth must immediately end. Population equilibrium is inevitable. The only questions are when and how. Stability will occur—by fewer births or more deaths.

That the day of reckoning eventually will come has been apparent for years. In 1798, Thomas Malthus foresaw the problem in a book, *Essay on the Principle of Population.* The theories that Malthus projected have long been a cornerstone of demographic thought.

Malthus identified one very important reality. He said that population increases in a geometrical ratio—2, 4, 8, 16 and so on—while food increases arithmetically—1, 2, 3, 4 and so on. Thus, he argued that the race between food and mouths inevitably would be lost. The only question would be when.

Malthus did not realize that science would make great headway in perfecting birth control methods, thus making possible the control of geometrical increase. But in a world where birth control is not practiced intelligently by two thirds of the population, Malthus' insight remains relevant.[17]

When Malthus was writing, the world population had not reached its first billion. That did not happen until 1830. By 1960, the population had climbed to three billion. The fourth billion was added in 15 years. The present rate of population increase is 1.9 percent a year, a rate that will double the population of the world in 36 years.[18]

The race between food and mouths is most graphically seen in the underdeveloped world. The prospects for Southeast Asia and portions of Latin America and Africa are dismal. In these countries the death rate already is rising. In many, population control will more likely come through premature deaths than by widespread contraception.[19]

Given present rates of growth, Southeast Asia will double its population in less than thirty years; Africa in twenty-seven years; and Latin America in twenty-four years. If these areas were to continue to double approximately every twenty-five years for a century, the population of the underdeveloped world would leap from the present 2.5 billion to 40 billion! But this will not happen. The world will not be able to support that population.

In many areas, such as Southeast Asia, the growth rate of urban areas is even higher. If Calcutta were to continue growing at its present rate, by the end of this century there would be sixty million people struggling for survival in that one city. A Malthusian nightmare!

The implications of this type of growth are staggering. The earth systems are under tremendous pressure. For example, if no per capita increase in food consumption is assumed, by soon after the year 2000 an additional one billion tons of grain a year will be needed. Such an amount is double the world's present output. But with increased consumption the need could rise to three billion tons a year.[20] While production of such large amounts of food may be possible, it would put a tremendous strain on already limited resources and environment.

Nor does anyone know what to do with the increase in the labor force that results from population growth. In South Asia, the potential labor force now grows by 350,000 people a week. By the end of the century that will have risen to 750,000 a week or 40 million a year, a number twice as large as the total present population of Canada.[21]

Why do "they" keep having so many children? One of the basic reasons is man's irrepressible will to survive. In many parts of the world, survival depends on having children to provide care during their parents' old age. Children are to people in developing countries what Social Security is to the elderly in this country. In many countries it is necessary to have eight to ten children to assure the survival of two or three. So the vicious cycle continues: more people, more hunger, more deaths, more people.

When children stand a better chance of survival, parents tend to have fewer of them. There is ample evidence that population decreases go hand in hand with improvements in the quality of life. Paradoxically, lowering the death rate by providing adequate diet and basic health care is one way to apply the brakes on population increase.

A number of poor countries have had some success in reducing the rate of population growth by assuring survival. In countries such as mainland China, Barbados, Sri Lanka, Uruguay, Taiwan, and South Korea, the birth rate has declined. The common denominator is that large portions of the population have gained access to economic benefits and increased security.

Birth control and family planning programs are also important though they seem to work well only in connection with programs of overall development. When increased security, however, creates the desire to have fewer children, family planning information becomes vital. Figures indicate that a third of the people in the world try to practice birth control. Half of those do so only by natural means and even then with little understanding of the reproductive process.

In most of Latin America, where the birth rates are the highest, population control programs are not widespread. One of the primary causes for this is the traditional refusal of the Roman Catholic Church to endorse such practices.

How many people will the earth hold? No one knows for sure. Estimates range from six to fifteen billion people. Everyone is guessing since it is unknown what technological breakthroughs may come in the years ahead. Survival, however, must not depend on speculative advances that may or may not come to pass. Birth rates, therefore, must come down. There is no alternative other than starvation and human suffering of unimagined dimensions.

The cupboard does not have to be bare in millions of homes around the world. The problems are significant but not impossible to overcome. There are solutions. If we have the will to overcome hunger, it can be done.

For Thought and Discussion

1. What do the terms *First, Second, Third* and *Fourth Worlds* mean? Which *World* do we live in? What is a *Most Seriously Affected* (MSA) country? In which categories do they exist?

2. What is *kwashiorkor? marasmus?* What causes these diseases? What would it be like to experience them? Describe it.

3. What is the basic difference between the Third and Fourth World countries and the First World countries in terms of economics? How has the economic gap affected food supply?

4. How do the consumption patterns of Americans affect the world food crisis? In what areas do we consume more than a "fair share"?

5. Who was Thomas Malthus? What predictions did he make that are being fulfilled today? What do his predictions mean for the future?

6
Is There a Way Out of This Mess?

A nutritional doomsday is not inevitable. Much can be done to improve conditions and to help the developing countries to become self-reliant. Not every country needs to be self-sufficient in food, but all need to be self-reliant in the sense that they are able to purchase food if they are unable to grow it.

Self-reliance, however, usually means that food production must be increased in that country. Food normally can be grown locally more inexpensively than it can be purchased.

More Yield or More Land

Essentially there are only two ways to increase food production. Either the yield on land currently being cultivated must be increased or new land must be put under cultivation.

Americans find it difficult to understand why production cannot be increased greatly in underdeveloped countries. "Why, if they would just do it like it is done here, production would skyrocket."

American agriculture has been successful. The United States is the breadbasket of the world. In 1975, United States farmers produced over 200 million metric tons of cereal grains out of a world total of 1.25 billion tons.[1] In 1976, world production should rise to 1.3 billion tons, almost all of the gain due to the anticipated increases in the North American crop. About 80 million tons will be exported, 50 percent of world grain trade.[2]

So why don't the poor countries use American methods to

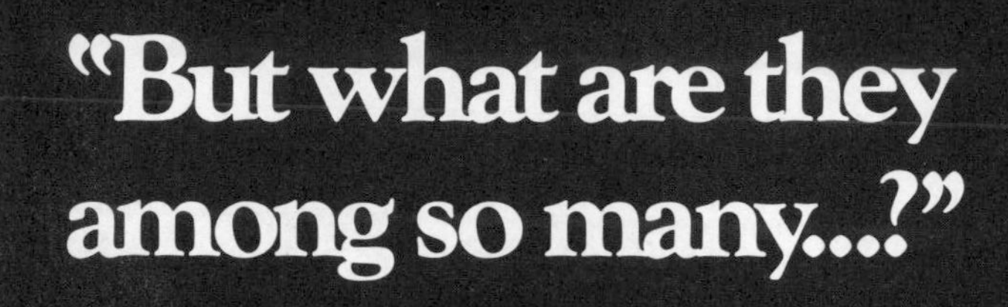
"But what are they
among so many...?"

increase production? Has not this country shared the necessary technology?

The technology has been shared. This country has had a strong interest in encouraging others to use our expertise. Whenever American methods are used abroad, substantial markets are opened up for fuel, fertilizer, and farm equipment.

The problem is that the way America farms is not necessarily how the rest of the world should farm. In fact, American methods may have created more problems than solutions for the developing countries.

American agriculture is based on big farms and big equipment. Farming is done by relatively few people using large amounts of capital, energy, fertilizer, and pesticides. The term often used to describe this approach is *capital-intensive.*

Capital-intensive agriculture has liabilities even in the United States. For one thing, ever-increasing amounts of fertilizer are required in order to maintain production. The amount of grain produced with each additional ton of fertilizer steadily diminishes.

The use of enormous amounts of pesticides causes serious ecological problems. Much of the world's fish production, for example, is threatened by concentration of pesticides in the shallow water estuaries where fish breed.

These problems, however, are small compared to the problems that the capital-intensive approach creates in less-developed countries. One of the devastating effects is that it takes people off the farm in countries where there is no other place to earn a living.

The underdeveloped countries of the world do not have alternate job possibilities. There is little industry. Thus, when a person is driven off the farm by "advanced technology," he usually faces a life of unemployment and poverty.

The necessity of avoiding a mass migration to the cities in

the developing countries has already been noted. In India, one hundred thousand people are being added to the labor force each week.[3] The cities simply do not have opportunities for such numbers of people.

In the less-developed countries, three fourths of the population lives off the land. Most of these countries are people-plentiful and land-short. They desperately need agricultural systems that emphasize people-power in the production of food. Such systems not only provide employment but also an environment that allows the expression of individual pride and initiative. Gradual industrialization then becomes more feasible as political and economic conditions are stabilized.

Such an approach, often described as *labor-intensive,* does not necessarily sacrifice productivity. On the contrary, there are several examples that indicate that small-plot production can exceed production on large farms. In India, per-acre yields on farms under five acres are 40 percent higher than on farms of more than fifty acres. Japan and Taiwan are other excellent examples of the production potential of small plots.[4]

Exported American agricultural techniques are burdened with other liabilities for developing countries. Extensive equipment is required, but most farmers do not have the capital to purchase it or the know-how to use and maintain it. Large amounts of fuel, fertilizer, and pesticides are also required, all of which are expensive. Fuel costs have skyrocketed; and the cost of petroleum-based fertilizers, though fluctuating, has followed closely behind.

Beyond American technology the other great hope for increased production has been the Green Revolution. Norman Borlaug, director of the Rockefeller Foundation's wheat breeding program in Mexico, is often identified as the father of the Green Revolution and was honored as such with the Nobel Peace Prize in 1970.

The beginnings, however, may go back as far as the late 1940s. Wheat genes developed by the Japanese were brought to the United States Department of Agriculture to use in developing more productive dwarf wheat varieties that would grow well in the United States. This *Gaines Wheat* was in turn used by Norman Borlaug in Mexico as the basis for new varieties that were amazingly adaptable to various growing conditions.

The dwarf wheats had several appealing characteristics. They were widely adaptable, very responsive to fertilizer and water, and matured early. But they were also capital-intensive, requiring large outlays for seeds, fertilizers, irrigation, and pesticides. These could be afforded by large farming operations but not by subsistence farmers. In Mexico, for example, the large wheat farmers benefited substantially from the new technology; but nearly 80 percent of Mexico's farmers are small farmers who grow corn. For them the Green Revolution has meant little.[5]

The scope of the Green Revolution has greatly expanded since Borlaug's work for which he received the Nobel Prize. Agricultural research has been intensified. Much of it is now being coordinated by the Consultative Group on International Agricultural Research. Founded in 1971, the Group sponsors research in a number of centers around the world. Emphasis is placed on tropical and arid-land agriculture and on crops for local use rather than crops for export. Intensive research is being done with such products as wheat, rice, potatoes, and livestock.

The future of the Green Revolution to some degree still is clouded in uncertainty. It is a failure, however, only if considered in the narrowest sense. Its earliest technology did benefit only a few; however, increased production by those few has at times prevented widespread disaster. Later research has resulted in improvements that are more universally usable. Scientists at the International Corn and Wheat Improvement Center in Mexico, for example, are trying to perfect a hybrid that would have the drought tolerance and disease resistance of barley, the self-fertilizing root system of the soybean, and the high yield and food value of wheat.[6]

Such research must continue. Man cannot rely on technology alone to bail him out of an ever-worsening situation. The solutions include much more than technological breakthroughs. Yet such breakthroughs are crucial and must be sought with an ear attuned to the social and agricultural realities of the developing world.

The other method for increasing production is to put more land under cultivation. Arid land that could be cultivated is available. In South America, much of the Amazon River basin could be farmed as could millions of acres across Central Africa. Some jungle lands in Indonesia, Malaysia, and Thailand could be used as well as the Mekong River basin in Southeast Asia.

The problem, however, is the enormous price involved in getting these lands into cultivation. Almost all of the easily cultivatable land in the world is being used. The tough cases are left, lands which theoretically are usable but which pose great obstacles to development.

In Africa, various diseases must be overcome before the use of some land is feasible. River blindness, malaria, and sleeping sickness present great difficulties. Control of the tsetse fly will be essential. In South America, tropical forests present a formidable barrier. In Asia, attempts have been made to cut down forests and create additional acreage, but the resulting increase in flooding and erosion has neutralized any gain.

The other possible source of substantial new food production is the sea. In recent years, however, nations have been fishing more and catching less. Strong competition has developed as sophisticated fishing fleets with fine-weave nets and on-board processing have ranged farther over the sea.

From 1950 to 1969, fish catches climbed steadily. Then, in

1970, catches began to decline and have been extremely erratic ever since. The primary cause for the drop is almost certainly overfishing. This decline means that catches of many table-grade fish may have reached maximum sustainable levels.

A case in point is the Peruvian anchovy fishery. By the early 1960s, Peru had become the world's leading fishing nation. The annual catch of anchovies rose steadily until it was running between ten and twelve metric tons in the early 1970s. Then, in 1972 and 1973, the anchovies seemed to disappear.

Studies indicated that the maximum sustainable anchovy yield was 9.5 million metric tons, and catches for several years had exceeded that level. Now the anchovies have begun to return, but the Peruvian government is exercising close control over fishing in order to give the stock opportunity to rebuild.[7]

The sea potentially can provide large amounts of needed protein for the world. International controls will be essential, however, to protect limited supplies of fish. The fish catch may even be increased substantially with fish farming and the harvesting of smaller fish such as krill, a small shellfish.

The catches, in turn, will need to be made available to the poorer countries at reasonable prices. For the most part, developing countries do not have sufficient capital for their own fishing industries even if they are fortunate enough to have ocean outlets.

People-Centered Development

Increased food production is part of the answer for the less developed countries. Even more fundamental, however, is long-term development that is directed toward creating ultimate self-sufficiency on the part of the people in the poorer countries.

Development has been defined by Edgar Stoesy as follows:

> Development is the process by which people are awakened to opportunities within their reach (conscientization). Development is people with

an increasing control over their environment and destiny. Development is people with dignity and a sense of self-worth. Development is freedom and wholeness and justice. Development is quality of life. Development is people living in the full realization of their God-given potential. Development is a liberated spirit. Development is people with rising expectations. Development is the new word for peace.[8]

Development is equipping people to care for themselves. At times it is almost synonymous with the giving of knowledge. Schumacher points this out. One helps a man a little by giving him a fish. Teach him to fish and he can help himself, then on a higher level:

Supply him with fishing tackle; this will cost you a good deal of money, and the result remains doubtful; but even if fruitful, the man's continuing livelihood will still be dependent on you for replacements. But teach him to make his own fishing tackle and you have helped him to become not only self-supporting but also self-reliant and independent.[9]

If this is an accurate definition of development, then development is needed at home as well as abroad. In a sense America has its own underdeveloped country in its midst. There are many in this country to whom the above language would sound hollow—the migrant workers who receive an annual average income of under $3,000; the 6 percent of national population who suffer from malnutrition; the elderly whose inflation-reduced income now buys beans if they are lucky, dog food if they are not. Development needs to begin at home. United States domestic policy like United States foreign policy has concentrated too much on relief and too little on development.

The distinction between relief and development must be understood. Relief is a term used for short-term help that is given in critical situations. Development refers to more lasting efforts directed toward helping people become self-sufficient.

There is general agreement today that a development approach should be taken whenever possible. It is to the advantage of both giver and recipient if the recipient is taught to help himself and is given the skills and resources to provide for himself.

Relief efforts, however, are necessary, also. The person who is suffering from the later stages of kwashiorkor, whose body has been reduced to a stumbling skeleton, cannot provide for himself. There are five hundred million hungry children in the world. They cannot provide for themselves. In these cases relief is necessary before long-term development efforts can even be considered.

In some cases relief also can be development, as in food-for-work programs where those who can do minimal labor are required to work on beneficial projects like wells or roads in return for life-sustaining food. Any response to world hunger, however, that does not include both relief and development stands on one leg. Both are necessary!

Effective development also must be people-centered rather than nation-centered. This means that it must get to the people who are most in need of help, those suffering from "absolute poverty."

It is at this point that development strategies utilized by the United States have failed. Generally the approach of this country has been the *trickle-down* theory of economic development. This theory is that if growth is stimulated at the top of the economic ladder, some of the benefits will *trickle-down* to those at the bottom of that ladder. Thus, for years, American governmental efforts have centered around helping the richest and most powerful individuals in developing countries to expand their interests. Especially favored were businesses that exploited raw materials and cheap labor and export businesses because these returned substantial benefits to this country. Rural development and projects for the poor were largely nonexistent.

The basic fallacy of *trickle-down* was that wealth failed to trickle. More was piled on the tables of the wealthy elites in developing countries, but bigger and better crumbs did not fall from the table for the benefit of the poor. In theory it seemed workable: stimulate economies, produce more jobs, and provide work for those in need. In practice, however, it did not work. Job opportunities did not begin to keep up with population growth, and wages often stayed at starvation levels. Consequently the bureaucrats and landowners cornered tremendous amounts of United States "assistance," and much of it wound up in Swiss bank accounts.

The Agency for International Development, the World Bank, and other agencies recently have evidenced significant shifts in policy in the direction of rural, labor-intensive development. There is encouraging evidence that such shifts may be an indication of basic, new approaches in United States development philosophy.

Meanwhile, the plight of the poor remains desperate. As Mooneyham points out,

> Studies by the World Bank indicate that in ten countries with per capita incomes averaging $145, the poorest 40 percent of the people receive a per capita income of only $50 a year. In another ten countries with per capita incomes averaging $275, the poorest 40 percent receive only $80. In India, some 200 million people subsist on incomes that average less than $40 a year.[10]

He does not say what the bottom 40 percent receive in countries like Bangladesh, Bhutan, Burma, Burundi, Chad, Mali, Rwanda, Somalia, and Upper Volta where the average per capita income is $80 or less!

The failure of development efforts to reach those most in need is not only the fault of the countries that are trying to provide assistance. It is due also to internal policies within the less developed countries.

Development is a two-way street. It depends on public and private resources being made available from external sources and on the determination, policies, and planning of the developing country. Long-range planning is essential and must be done primarily by the developing country, for only that country can determine goals and make the policy decisions necessary to implement those goals. Effective development is complex. It requires balancing and interrelating the answers to many questions. What are the cultural problems? What are the religious problems? What information is available from agronomists, hydrologists, agriculturalists, and other experts? What is the market for goods? What are the transportation problems? What materials are available and at what cost? What are the weather trends? What projects are most urgently needed? These and a hundred other considerations go into the makeup of an effective program of development.

Trade Policies That Help the Poor

Another essential ingredient in any recipe for successful development is trade balance. If a country consistently experiences heavy deficit trade balances, then capital must be used to offset that imbalance rather than being available for internal improvement efforts.

In recent years exports have accounted for approximately 80 percent of the total inflow of foreign exchange of developing countries.[11] But international trade is not working to the advantage of the less developed countries. Rather it is balancing out heavily in favor of the developed countries. In trade between the United States and Fourth World countries in 1975, the United States exported $4,138 million and imported $2,005 million, leaving the Fourth World countries $2,133 million poorer in trade relations with only one developed country.[12]

One significant reason for the growing trade deficit between the United States and the Fourth World has been the increased cost of cereal grains. The deficit is more a result of government nonpolicies than government policies. The agricultural market in the United States is largely beyond public scrutiny. It is dominated by five companies–Cargill, Continental, Cook Industries, Bunge, and Louis Dreyfuss–only one of which is publicly owned.

America now has no national food policy. At times this lapse of responsibility does not lead to human disaster. In the case of some Russian wheat purchases, however, the unwillingness of the government to exercise any control put both the American consumer and many American farmers at a disadvantage. In addition, millions of hungry people abroad were forced to pay premium prices for food or starve to death.

Some type of trade stabilization is necessary if Third and Fourth World countries are ever to have any hope of projecting long-term development efforts. To ensure economic security, either price-stabilization, which is advocated by developing countries, or earnings-stabilization, advocated by the United States, is necessary.

Another area in which trade reform is needed is liberalization of tariff barriers. For years the United States and other developed countries have erected tight tariff barriers against the importing of agricultural, processed, or manufactured goods from underdeveloped countries. The reason for the barriers was to protect American manufacturers from competition. One result was to discourage industrialization in underdeveloped countries. This in turn kept them trading in raw commodities that traditionally have large price fluctuations. It also kept underdeveloped countries dependent on other countries for processed or manufactured goods, thus creating markets for more advanced nations.

The impact of these trade policies has been to assure that

developing countries will have trade deficits in relation to developed countries. This has significantly perpetuated underdevelopment.

These policies currently are being discussed in a number of international forums, the main ones being UNCTAD IV (the fourth session of the United Nations Conference on Trade and Development) and GATT (General Agreement on Tariffs and Trade). The United States has made some significant proposals including the dismantling of much of the present developed-country tariff system of protection. Such liberalization of trade policies would benefit the consumer in the wealthy nations as well as the producer in the poor nations. It would assure an increased flow of cheaper imports. A small number of Americans would lose their jobs as a result. Government funds could be allocated to help restrain and relocate such persons.

Finally, the private sector plays a significant role in development. Private relief and development efforts have long been engaged effectively in helping the poor. Not only do such agencies provide food relief in critical areas, but also they are engaged in long-term development projects. Representatives of such agencies may be found supervising food-for-work programs, digging wells, organizing irrigation projects, reseeding pastures and forest land, and teaching farmers and herders improved methods of production.

Nongovernmental relief agencies generally have good records for effective work. Many of them deliver 90 percent or more of every donated dollar to people in need. The efforts of such agencies frequently are directed at helping the poorest of the poor.

In 1974, private voluntary assistance by citizens of the United States was $735 million. This was the equivalent of $3.47 for each person in the country.[13]

Business That Gives as Well as Receives

Private investment also is an important, if controversial, factor in development. Private capital indeed may be one of the most determinative factors in the developing world. The question is whether it will be a factor in development or in economic plunder.

The huge business conglomerates, the MNC's (multinational corporations), are being referred to accurately as the newest form of international government. Their economic influence often can spell success or failure for improvement efforts in developing countries. The MNC's can bring needed resources, skills, and training. They can also embody a new form of economic colonialism, extracting from developing countries far more capital and resources than they invest.

Most developing countries continue to want MNC's to locate within their borders, but the "rules of the game" are becoming increasingly strict. Countries are sensitive to the fact that decisions in the headquarters of corporations are made on the basis of what serves the interest of that corporation rather than what serves the interest of the local people. Frequently the two come into conflict.

The developing countries have other areas of concern. Corporations are buying and renting large amounts of land in poor countries. This land is turned to producing high-cash crops instead of needed foodstuffs. In Colombia, for example, the wheat grown on a hectare (approximately two and a half acres) will bring about 12,000 pesos, but carnations grown for export might bring a million pesos.[14] Thus land that may be needed for food production is turned to producing crops that benefit no one except stockholders and the few who are given jobs.

Another area of concern is corporate advertising. In search of new markets, MNC's have come into some underdeveloped countries with strong advertising campaigns that create appetites for goods that are not needed or, in some instances, are actually harmful. In one country, advertising campaigns to sell milk formulas to mothers who had no refrigeration or sterilization facilities had disastrous consequences.

Multinational corporations can provide some benefits to developing countries. Agreements are going to be necessary, however, on both home-country and host-country policies concerning the activities of foreign investors.

Increased production, effective development, fair trade policies, and responsible investment are all key ingredients for recovery in the underdeveloped world. Like pieces of a puzzle, they must fit together. If any of the pieces are missing, the result will be a picture of continued human suffering.

For Thought and Discussion

1. What are the two basic ways to increase food production? Which seems to be the most realistic method? Why do poor countries have difficulty farming by the American method? What is the difference between *capital-intensive* and *labor-intensive* farming?

2. What food sources are available other than from farm land? What is the potential for *farming* the sea?

3. What is *development?* How should America be involved in development? What is the difference between relief and development? What is meant by *people-centered* development? How can it be encouraged?

4. How do our nation's trade policies affect the food crisis? How do our trade policies need to be reformed? What impact would it have?

5. How can businesses help concerning the food shortage? What are the concerns of the developing countries in regard to the multinational corporations? What changes need to be made by the large international companies as they relate to the poor nations?

7
The Earth Is the Lord's–or Is It?

In gatherings of scientists it is not uncommon for participants to be pessimistic about the future of human life. Some serious students suggest that in less than two hundred years the human species will be extinct. If they are right and the human race has been in existence for one million years, then it would mean that humankind has finished over 99 percent of its life expectancy.

One does not have to accept this dim outlook to agree that prospects for the future are not bright. As man endangers the life of other species, he himself becomes one of the endangered species.

What this generation is doing to the environment has become a focal point of social concern. On one hand, alarmists see man choking to death on his own waste and warn that time is very short to avert worldwide disaster. On the other hand, debunkers insist that the quality of life is threatened but that survival is not the question. Various of these optimists see hope in the restorative processes of nature, technology, global cooperation, or some religious loophole in the laws of the universe.

The truth of the matter is probably somewhere between the views of the doomsdayers who see the end at hand and the deniers who see no real problems with the environment. To find the truth of the matter, then, becomes important business. No intelligent person can ignore the question of what is happening to the environment.

This generation has had dumped in its lap the awareness of the interrelatedness of all aspects of the environment. Everything is related to everything else. When man tries to take anything out of nature by itself, he discovers it hitched to everything else in the universe. This means that we never change merely one thing. When we tamper with one part of the system, we discover that we upset the delicate balance of the total system. This is the essence of ecology.

Ecology suddenly becomes more important. It is the study of the balance of all living things in nature. The total of all the living and nonliving parts that support a chain of life in a specific area is called an *ecosystem.*

The growing demand for food has pushed mankind to the limits in his treatment of these ecosystems. He is now messing with the fine tuning that will really throw the picture out of kilter.

The ecosystems that together make up the entire earthly scene are in jeopardy. This world is seen as a fragile spacecraft, a closed system with limited resources for its journey. It has a breathable atmosphere less than ten miles tall and useful soil only a few inches deep. Only 3 percent of the earth's water is fresh, and most of that is in the polar ice caps. The flow of silent violence against our common environment threatens human existence.

Ecology sounds a severe warning. Hold everything! E. F. Schumacher puts it well.

> Ecology holds 'that an environmental setting developed over millions of years must be considered to have some merit.' Anything so complicated as a planet, inhabited by more than a million and a half species of plants and animals, all of them living together in a more or less balanced equilibrium in which they continuously use and re-use the same molecules of the soil and air, cannot be improved by aimless and uninformed tinkering.[1]

Spaceship earth moves forward with a natural interdependence of all things on it. That interdependence is in process, alive, happening now. From a Christian point of view this ongoing creation is all inclusive, a package deal. The Creator himself would have it that way. It was he who programmed this interdependence.

And it is good.

Danger Signals

What has brought to a head the awareness of ecological danger? The particular problems that have sounded the alarm are varied.

1. *The specter of used up nonrenewables* has jolted awake many who slept. For a mineral to be used up frightens thinking people. The shortage of petroleum hit hard at hungry lands. Nitrogen fertilizers are a petroleum by-product. Pesticides are made from crude oil. Gasoline and diesel powered pumps keep water flowing in irrigation systems. The knowledge that selfishness and greed contribute to resource scarcity has made an impact. For instance, the people of the United States waste as much in energy resources as people in Japan use. Most of that waste is in fossil fuels that can never be replaced.

2. *Individual responsibility for ecology* is dawning on some persons in the developed nations. The average American is catching on that he himself is–consciously or unconsciously–a part of the problem. The words of Fritz Kreisler have meaning. "I am constantly endeavoring to reduce my needs to the minimum. I feel morally guilty in ordering a costly meal, for it deprives someone else of a slice of bread, some child, perhaps, a bottle of milk."[2]

3. *The costliness of ecological change* is becoming apparent. Pollution control, new energy sources, and land reclamation are expensive. To save the earth will be costly, not only economically

but also in terms of forsaking old ways and traditions. Nothing less than a startling break with past patterns will be enough to make a difference.

4. *The madness of consumerism* is becoming clearer in the light of world hunger. The unrestrained, unbounded pursuit of goods does not harmonize with ecological concern. Consumption for consumption's sake is destructive at every level. Consumerism is directly related to pollution of the environment and robbery of those with the greatest needs. The average American produces about six pounds of solid waste a day or about a ton each year. A consumer culture aims at developing buying habits that turn consumers into wasteful, debt-ridden, and perpetually discontented persons.

5. *The fear of overpopulation* has become a matter of international concern. The more people there are, the more pollution of every sort. The greater the number of persons, the greater is the load on the ecosystems.

6. *The rapidity of change* has shocked persons into consideration of the future. The changes that endanger this good earth, its air, water, and soil have not been as frightening as the rate of destruction.

7. *Floods, earthquakes, droughts* have made headlines. Other natural environmental phenomena have also created disasters upsetting the ecology of entire nations and bringing starvation to millions. Bangladesh, Honduras, Guatemala, and the growing edge of the Sahara desert known as the Sahel have all offered laboratory demonstrations of massive death due to ecological disaster. Starvation comes to thousands when environmental change, even relatively slight, upsets an ecology that barely provides for life.

8. *The undermining of food systems* can be done by men as well as by natural causes. This comes in many ways:

—the destruction of vegetation

—deforestation
—land mismanagement
—loss of topsoil
—overloading the land with humans or livestock beyond its carrying capacity
—overfishing
—overfertilization of fresh water bodies with either commercial or animal fertilizers
—industrial waste pollution of fresh waters
—destruction of marshlands.

Ironically, man in his ingenuity has engaged in all of these and dozens of other practices that effectively limit food production in an already hungry world. Men keep tinkering with the God-given ecological mechanism that might make enough food if supported rather than exploited.

9. *The growth of cities* is closely related to the preceding ecological dangers. It is happening all over the world. Land is taken out of production. Consumers multiply while food producers disappear. Wastemakers become more skilled at destruction of the environment. The internal combustion engine fouls the air. More water is needed. Urbanization brings all of these features and more to the environment. The mushrooming of urban areas continues to destroy ecosystems.

Conflict

Environmental problems are even more complicated than the list of warning signals above would indicate. The developing nations of the world are experiencing two types of environmental pressures. One is concerned with protecting nature and its ecosystems. The other is more concerned with the social ecosystems that are producing hunger.

Among hungry peoples the ecological question is not as simple as a struggle for a clean environment and the limitation of resource use and waste. No, in many lands that are fighting hunger the environmental question becomes a battle between the rights of nature and the rights of humanity. The nature environmentalists work for better air and water while the poverty environmentalists press for jobs and food.

In poor nations the immediate need for food outweighs the long-range need to preserve the environment. The leaders of hungry people have to consider avoiding dangerous pesticides, harmful fertilizers, and destructive irrigation systems while they press for increased agricultural production. It is not difficult to understand their dilemma. Poor nations are being asked to pay a price for clean environment that rich nations did not bother to pay while they became rich.

Art Simon in his magnificent book *Bread for the World* points out that "pollution-free hunger" does not appeal to the poor of the world. They may logically "conclude that 'protecting the environment' is another name for staying hungry."[3] The interdependence of life that is the basis of ecology includes, first of all, the life of people. True concern with the environment includes freedom from hunger.

Environmental problems, especially for poor nations, involve conflicts between economic efficiency and ecological sanity. The same tension exists in more developed nations. The necessity of such a trade-off is particularly sad and unpleasant with the blackmail of starvation stalking the streets.

The desperation of the search for solutions to the environmental crisis may lead to other dangers. Overreaction and oversimplified answers to the threats to nature could cause man to become more and more dependent on the false god: superscience. He could turn to totalitarian forms of government because they promise quick answers. Man could accept such a pessimistic world view that he would go along with murderous power brokering by the strong nations. A sort of conspiratorial, passive genocide could be practiced, destroying by neglect the poorest of the world's peoples.

Scientific inventiveness cannot solve any and all of man's needs as he depletes his natural resources. The worship of science–scientism–is a prevalent form of idolatry. Totalitarianism and narrow nationalism also tend to take the place of God in the lives of many persons who do not know a God who created the environment, sustains the ecosystems, and cares for the hungry. The God revealed in the Bible offers a live option to the bleak ecological picture. Those who trust that God share a lively hope that ecological progress can be made.

Positive Responses

Concern for ecological imbalance is old. The Old Testament evidences an interest in the environment. Some passages sound strangely modern (Num. 35:33-34; Isa. 24:4-6).

Approaches to stop the drift toward environmental destruction must be imaginative. A variety of answers must be given to the question, What can avert ecological death? These answers are of different types, different weights, on different levels of response. Some portions of this answer list are more scientific while others are more political. Some items listed are general, others more specific. Almost all of them have implications for the individual. Every suggestion is practical.

1. *Develop an interdisciplinary approach.* Threats to the very existence of our life-support systems have tended to bring people together. The gaps between groups are being bridged by a common concern for the future of the human race. This kind of cooperation is essential. Separate solutions to portions of our environmental ills will only make matters worse.

2. *Work toward global cooperation.* The environment does not observe political boundaries. Ecosystems know no racial or ethnic lines. The United Nations, the World Bank, the Overseas Devel-

opment Council, Bread for the World, and the churches are all working on hunger and ecology as a *world* problem.

3. *Recognize the need for balanced growth.* Only with some sort of leveling off of growth can the environment be salvaged. This immediately suggests that some nations, industries, areas, and so forth, will grow less while others will be helped to grow more. If harmony with nature and justice for people are both to be secured, discriminate, not helter-skelter, growth must come. Trade-offs will not be easy. Economic and political accommodation to human hunger will not please everyone. Yet if the environment is to sustain human life on earth and if hungry people are to be fed, tough choices about the distribution of wealth will be made.

4. *Use well all natural resources.* Land, water and air must be protected for tomorrow. New land use policies will emerge at every level of government. Deserts will be reclaimed. Air and water will be cleaned up. Limited natural resources will be guarded. The need is clear for careful resource management for the good of all, for future generations.

5. *Support life-giving research.* Solar and thermal energy, medical research, agricultural studies, population control, educational techniques for developing nations, labor-intensive industry, practical transportation, housing improvement, and dozens of other areas beg for substantial research now. More monies should be made available for this type of life-giving study in contrast to the death-producing military expenditures.

6. *Move toward a disciplined consumerism.* There is room for progress when 5 percent of the world's people (all in the United States) consume more marketable wealth than the poor 70 percent of the world's people. Maybe we will use less "disposable" stuff. Maybe we will reexamine our needs and be more sparing, less materialistic.

7. *Educate for action.* At home, at school, and at church

ecology education for the young and consciousness raising for those not so young should be routine. But the education needed is not an academic sort; it is training to help bring about changed attitudes and changed lives in relation to the environment. The targets of this teaching range from conservation of water and energy to good nutrition without waste.

8. *Press for government action.* Church and civic groups can insist upon tax reform, government accountability to the public, a responsive legislative process, and affirmative action on ecological concerns.

9. *Redefine progress.* With a lower level of growth in some areas, vocational direction and the definition of success will change. Progress may not always mean more and bigger products, budgets, outputs, buildings, and sales. Greater production may not be greater at all.

The advocates of change or progress who oppose environmentalists should bear the burden of proof. The environmentalist or ecologist should no longer have to prove that the "progress," proposed change, or development will do harm. The person pushing a project or product, a development or design should have to test it and show without a doubt that it will advance human priorities humanely.

10. *Offer a model of cooperation.* The church can demonstrate interdependence if anyone can. Christians should remember Acts 2 and the pattern set by the early church. The very word for fellowship, *koinonia,* should take on new meaning for today as churches model for the world what it means to care for one another.

For too long a prodigal society has wasted its substance. It is time for us to come to our senses and arise.

The heavy agenda above demands changed minds. Ecological problems will not be settled without new attitudes.

The ecological issue is at its base a religious issue. Since ecology demands a radical, new outlook, it calls for a radically fresh religion. What people do about ecosystems will be determined by what they think about themselves, their relation to things, and their own nature and destiny. These are all religious questions. It is urgent, then, for the church to become an ecological conscience. Life and breath depend upon it.

If change is needed in the way man sees his life and the world around him—and it is—no group is better equipped to bring it; no element of society has more to offer than the Christian church. What does the church have to offer?

Toward a Christian Ecology

The church presses toward the ultimate unity of all things in God (Col. 1:17). Christians share a vision of a new heaven and a new earth. These beliefs impinge upon the present order at several points.

1. *A philosophy of reality.* Biblical Christianity sees the world as objectively real. Nature and history are not illusions, ideas, or dreams. They are the stuff of life and are to be taken seriously. Real religion involves regard for man's welfare in this real world, not just concern for his eternal salvation. Because Western thought has been built largely upon Christian presuppositions, modern science could develop. Science had to have a world that was real and relatively reliable.

2. *A value for nature.* The world around us is not merely a stage upon which man struts out his role. Nature has worth and value on its own. The biblical writers never saw nature as merely a useful tool. The earth witnesses to the glory of God, and God delights in his work. God has made the beautiful and wonderful as well as the necessary stuff of life (Ps. 104). This worth is derived from its createdness. The value of things is drawn from and related to the God who made them, as is man's dignity and worth.

3. *A theology for ecosystems.* A Christian understanding of God sees him concerned with all of nature, man's life, and everything that touches it. Theology at its best is capable of redefining the man-nature relationship to include a view of nature as an instrument of God's grace. Christian theology recognizes the worth of nature as an object of God's love and redemptive purposes. God holds it all together. Without him creation would revert to chaos (Job 34:14-15; Ps. 104:29-30). One can make better sense of the world by understanding that God makes it cohere. God's purpose for creation is one of redemption (Col. 1:17).

4. *An ethic for change.* A sense of what ought to be springs from being in touch with God's redemptive purposes. Christian ethics encompasses man in relation to his neighbor and to the social order. It also deals with man in his relation to creatures and things living and nonliving. Christians are, indeed, custodians of God's redemptive purpose, communicators of his grace, guardians of a sense of oughtness. They are and can be no less than stewards of the realities of earth. Their pilgrimage toward a heavenly home does not justify their abusing, wasting, or uglying this one while they are here. It is a sad thing that Christians have sung "This world is not my home" with such obvious glee. They may be temporary tenants, but they should care for the dwelling.

5. *An approach to management.* The above ethic is built upon a stewardship concept. There has never been any such thing as unlimited rights or unhindered freedom for God's children. Some critics see Genesis 1:28 (replenish the earth and subdue it . . . have dominion) as the historical ground for a bulldozer mentality. This passage has never been a license to exploit nature. Rather, the Bible makes it clear that man is responsible for the wise use of resources. (See chapter 2). There have been limitations and priorities on the biblical mandate from the be-

ginning (Gen. 2:15). Mankind has a stewardship responsibility to his borrowed world. A thorough study of the Bible shows that nothing is man's. Yet much of his history reveals man treating his natural heritage as if nothing were God's. Man as manager of God's possessions is a correct stance regarding nature. This attitude may also serve as a check on his selfishness and greed.

6. *A motive for action.* A right understanding of stewardship alone will not get man to do the right thing. Only *agape* love, grounded in God, whose very being is love (1 John 4:8) is good enough to move persons to sustained action. To will the welfare of all creatures and things is the basic principle of Christian behavior and the essence of ethics. Francis A. Schaeffer makes it plain.

> If I love the Lover, I love what the Lover has made. Perhaps this is the reason why so many Christians feel an unreality in their Christian lives. If I don't love what the Lover has made—in the area of man, in the area of nature—and really love it because He made it, do I really love the Lover at all?[4]

7. *An overview for perspective.* A Christian approach, precisely because it does have a world view, offers a dimension of wholeness not brought to ecology by some approaches. Ecology by definition must rest on a holistic assumption. Man in all his relationships is touched by God's love. The heavenly Father wills the well-being of all creation. The ancient greeting *shalom* speaks of the holistic commitment. Again Schaeffer makes it clear.

> So, if nature and the things of nature are only a meaningless series of particulars in a decreated universe, with no universal to give them meaning, then nature is become absurd, wonder is gone from it—and wonder is equally gone from me, because I too am a finite thing.
>
> But Christians insist that we do have a universal, God is there![5]

Now that offers a working basis for ecological balance.

8. *A respect for things.* A biblical theme often repeated is an

awareness of God's presence in the world (Ps. 19,24,121). This consciousness lends itself to wonder and awe. A healthy, reverent appreciation for all of life is appropriate. Yet Christians are not pantheists. God and his handiwork are not to be equated (1 Tim. 4:4). What God has made is not God himself. Schaeffer has stated a Christian understanding of the God-nature relationship.

> God treats His creation with integrity: each thing in its own order, each thing the way He made it. If God treats His creation in that way, should we not treat our fellowcreature with a similar integrity? If God treats the tree like a tree, the machine like a machine, the man like a man, shouldn't I, as a fellow creature do the same?[6]

God alone possesses true independence and absolute autonomy. He is Creator and Sustainer. His creation and sustenance give meaning and integrity to all he has made.

Beyond the dignity with which the natural order is endowed by God's creative work, the incarnation lifts higher the meaning of all that God has made. By being a part of the actual patterns of human life, Jesus Christ made special not only humanity but also the whole web of life. The Christian, then, places a high value on the material creation. He respects God's handiwork.

9. *A special place for mankind.* Though all creation has meaning and integrity, man is different (Gen. 1:27; Ps. 8; John 3:16; Jas. 3:10). Persons are more than things. Every generation of Christians has its own version of the "I am nothing" crazies. It is a biblical heresy to deny one's own worth. When one is made in God's image and bought with the blood of Jesus Christ, his value is clear from the view of biblical revelation.

Persons are worth more than things. No human being is merely a collection of atoms. The rights of persons are to be set above the rights of property. There is a hierarchy of value in God's creation with humankind at the top of the pyramid.

In spite of all that, each person is a bundle of atoms, a part of the created, in some ways one with nature. Each one of us has a special affinity with all mankind. We are of "one blood" (Acts 17:26) and in touch with the natural processes just as every other person (Matt. 5:45).

10. *A hope for the future.* God is on the side of health and wholeness. He is at work for good in all of this as he has always been. The Christian faith is moving forward with a theology of hope (Heb. 13:8). A new wave of Christian thought has come from the future-oriented theologians. (Among them are Jürgen Moltmann and Wolfhart Pannenberg.) Henlee Barnette comments on their note of hope. "They say little about nature as such, but they do take history seriously, stress hope, envision the unity of the whole world, and see the Kingdom of God pressing proleptically from the future into the present with transforming power.[7]

A Christian ecology has much to offer in the present crisis. It must be hammered out now.

World hunger endangers the human species. Death follows apathy. Christians and those who share their vision will act. Deuteronomy 30:19 draws the line. "I have set before you life and death, blessing and cursing: therefore choose life, that both thou and thy seed may live."

For Thought and Discussion

1. What is ecology? an ecosystem?

2. Why is there conflict between those who would protect nature and some who would produce more food? How can that conflict be resolved?

3. What are some ways we are encouraged to buy things that you do not really want or need? How can we change buying habits?

4. What have you seen in the newspapers or magazines within this week that speaks of the destruction of ecosystems? of the relationship of that destruction to world hunger?

5. How does Christianity speak to ecological concerns? What do you believe Christians should do about ecology?

8
What Do You Mean, One World?

Political involvement is an essential ingredient in any recipe for an effective response to world hunger. Political decisions have far more impact on mankind than all private relief and development efforts.

The neglect of personal political responsibility surrenders to ignorance and indifference. It encourages political powers to draw the wrong conclusions and to make the wrong decisions. To fail to make feelings known about critical decisions is worse than bad citizenship. It is sin. It is simply a more sophisticated way of walking on the other side of the road, ignoring the one who suffers. It is a clear evidence, a testimony, of unconcern. As such, it is a denial of God. It is as telling, if not as articulate, as Peter's denial by the campfire. God is love. To care for others is to affirm God. Not to care is to deny him.

Neighbor is defined geographically too often. The Christian understanding of neighbor-love is neither provincial nor geographical; it is vital and all-encompassing. It has no national or racial boundaries. Nor can limits be placed on the modes of authentic expression of that love. It is both direct to the neighbor who is near and indirect to the neighbor who is faraway. It is expressed by word and authenticated by deed. Its political expression is invalid without personal expression, and its personal expression is invalid without political expression. Thus to ignore political involvement is more than bad citizenship; it is bad Christianity.

"Much is required..."

To plead powerlessness is a contemporary cop-out, a half-truth that can become truth only if people believe it. People-power has been suppressed by the bigness of government and economic superpowers, but it has not been removed. It ultimately dies by nonuse, a form of political suicide rather than assassination.

The quest is for justice, Micah expressed it, "He hath shewed thee, O man, what is good; and what doth the Lord require of thee, but to do justly, and to love mercy, and to walk humbly with thy God?" (Micah 6:8).

The Christian is a political realist, but his actions are controlled by prophetic conscience as well as political reality. His political hope is not rooted in scientific, economic, or political analysis but in the faith that the kingdom of God is the ultimate reality and that the power of God goes beyond the power of men. With that understanding he can live with integrity in the political context. And it is in the political context that Christians must be prepared to move if they are to have a significant impact on the plight of suffering humanity.

Effective political involvement presupposes an understanding of the issues and of the goals that one is seeking to achieve. What are the goals or values that should be sought within the international order? Movement toward a just world would surely be one such goal, but even that does not encompass enough. Ecological balance, increased economic well-being, and the maximization of human freedom might be other legitimate ends to be pursued.

A New International Scene

Whatever the articulation of goals, it is obvious that the international ball game is being played in a totally new ball park. Old things, indeed, have passed away. Behold, all things are becoming new. Signs that the world system is going through radical transformation are all about. Even the language is new, with such words as *interdependence, new world order, global survival bargains, self-reliance,* and *international economic order* becoming necessary parts of an informed vocabulary. Experts in international affairs are saying that the mid-1970s mark the end of one era and the beginning of another. Geoffrey Barraclough has said that what is happening is "the opening stage of a struggle for a new world order, a search for positions of strength in a global realignment, in which the weapons (backed, naturally, by the ultimate sanction of force) are food and fuel."[1]

As this search for a new world order begins, what are the dominant characteristics of the international scene? First, there is growing recognition that this spaceship earth, on which mankind lives, has certain *ultimate limitations.* Earth systems can become overloaded. A waste-saturated environment already poses problems, and further accelerated deterioration seems inevitable.

Mineral resources, many of them vital to present life-styles and methods of production, rapidly are being exhausted. Many of these resources are nonrenewable.

The world is running out of cheap energy. If all nations used petroleum at the rate the developed world uses it, all reserves would be used up by 1892. Even with new discoveries made at the current rate, reserves would be depleted by 1985. Effective petroleum substitutes will not be available by then. The result is clear.

> The industrialized world is thus granted the time to develop alternative energy sources only by using nearly the entire world oil reserves and by that action preempting the supply of the most efficient and convenient energy source precisely when the developing nations need it most.[2]

The developed nations of the world are insisting that the 2.5 percent population growth rate of the developing world be reduced. Would it not also be appropriate for the developing countries to insist that the 4 percent annual increase in the use of energy by developed countries be curtailed?

Another characteristic of the contemporary international scene is *shifting alignments.* In many ways "East-West" alignments are changing to "North-South" alignments. The developed world lies almost totally to the north of the equator while the underdeveloped world lies to the south. The determination to maintain comparable life-styles at the expense of other countries may cause alliances between countries that in the past have been politically incompatible.

New alliances built around economic interest already have begun to play a prominent role in international affairs. OPEC, the Organization of Petroleum Exporting Countries, has become a significant international force. OPEC, in turn, may spawn other such alliances. There already is indication that OPEC countries may direct large sums of their new wealth into financing other developing country power blocs.

Tensions have continued to grow between OPEC and OECD (the Organization for Economic Cooperation Development). OECD is the First World answer to the Third World OPEC.

A third factor in the present scene is an increased resort to *political repression* and the corresponding loss of personal freedom. There has been a steady increase in the number of authoritarian regimes, inevitably leading to suppression of the free press and academic freedom. Some military regimes actually have engaged in efforts to eliminate the intellectual elite within the country. The 1974 Freedom House Annual World Survey listed 61 countries and territories as free, 67 as partly free and 77 as not free. The Survey defines freedom as the existence of political and civil rights.

Intensive armament is another characteristic of the international situation. Nearly every nation is walking around now with a gun on each hip. Weapons are more widely dispersed than ever before, and the destructive capability of individual governments has increased substantially. The nuclear club is growing. Six nations—the United States, Great Britain, France, the Soviet Union, China, and India—are now definite members. At least eight other nations have produced or are capable of producing nuclear weapons, and approximately thirty others are capable of making atomic weapons within one to five years.[3]

Several years ago the United States was spending close to $250 million a day for military purposes. That amount exceeded the total annual budget of the United Nations World Food Program and was twice the amount of the combined annual budgets of the World Health Organization and the Food and Agriculture Organization.[4]

America is not the only country with heavy military expenditures. Several Third World countries commit heavy portions of their limited budgets to military spending. In India, where thousands are starving on the streets, one third of the budget goes to the military. In Egypt, a country with increasing hunger, one fourth of the national budget goes for military purposes.

America is also the gunrunner of the world. In 1974, American companies sold more than eight billion dollars of military hardware. The present figure exceeds ten billion dollars. Advanced, sophisticated weapons frequently are sold to both sides of international conflicts.[5] Moral considerations seldom are taken into account. Too often the rationale is, "If we do not sell weapons to them, someone else will." The same argument is made by drug pushers.

"Blessed are the peacemakers: for they shall be called the children of God" (Matt. 5:9). Many contend that world peace demands a reduction in arms trade. The United States, it is said, should lead the way in arms limitation. Does this mean, however, that the country would be left defenseless and open to attack? That argument is ridiculous.

Obviously it is imperative that this nation be able to defend itself. The decision not to be conservative in military spending was made long ago. The decision now is whether to encourage insane levels of expenditures that would give this country the absurd capacity to kill everyone in the world over and over.

The United States is not out-gunned. In 1974, the United States had 8,500 strategic nuclear bombs deployed, nearly 40 for every city of 100,000 in the Soviet Union. The Soviet Union had 2,800 such bombs. The United States also has deployed 22,000 tactical nuclear bombs. The United States deploys another "nuclear device" on the average of one every eight hours while the Soviet Union deploys one every forty-eight hours. There is the equivalent of over 600,000 Hiroshima bombs in the United States arsenal, enough firepower to kill everyone in the world fifty times.

What does this have to do with hunger? Money spent for weapons in any part of the world cannot be spent to battle the social problems that challenge mankind. Overkill and underfeed go together. Soon after becoming President, Dwight Eisenhower said: "Every gun that is made, every warship launched, every rocket fired signifies in the final sense, a theft from those who hunger and are not fed, those who are cold and are not clothed."[6]

The growth of the conglomerates, the *multi-national corporations*, is another significant development on the international scene. A part of the "sixth continent" (intergovernmental, nongovernmental, and business organizations that basically operate independent of national boundaries), the MNC's are rapidly dislodging states in the global power struggle. Lists of world centers of power consistently include from fifteen to twenty corporations in the top fifty power centers. Because these MNC's owe their primary allegiance to their own welfare rather than to a particular state; and because they remain relatively uncontrolled in the international sector, they operate internationally with a frightening amount of independence.

Mass human suffering is another reality that must be dealt with in any discussion of foreign policy. In many countries the most urgent task is simple to state but difficult to accomplish: provide food for starving people. International relations boil down to the ratio between mouths and manna, and anything beyond that is to some degree unessential. The battle against endemic poverty and chronic malnutrition claims nearly all the resources and energies that many peoples possess. In recent years some countries have had to assume heavy debt burdens to purchase food and food-producing products. These debt burdens, in turn, have forced them to adopt policies that further impoverished their people, such as expanding agricultural exports to meet debt payments instead of keeping the food to meet domestic food shortages.[7] Any foreign policy that at its core places a high value on human life must consider whether policies will increase or decrease human suffering.

Finally, it has become obvious that the interrelationship between nations is developing into a web of *mutual dependencies. Interdependence* has become the catchword to describe this contemporary reality. It has become the dominant image, the focal point of discussion about the world community. It is adhered to, at least superficially, by nearly all international factions.

Nations, all nations, are becoming more dependent on each other. Interdependence, however, must not be equated with equality or mutual dependence. Many nations still are far more dependent than others. Their bargaining position is essentially inferior, a fact not altered by the rhetoric of independence. Interdependence rightly understood and applied leads to cooperative efforts that further global justice.

International Developments

Like a ball rolling downhill, international developments rapidly have been picking up speed in recent years. Especially in the last ten years changes have come with disturbing rapidity. A look at some of the recent highlights is helpful to provide a context for current understanding.

The Group of 77. The North-South debate began to take shape in the late 1950s as a group of Southern countries began to avoid alliances with both the Communist and Western blocs of nations. This already mentioned alliance was known as the "*Group of 77,*" or Third World. These countries tried to present a united front to other bargaining powers. They pressed for various kinds of reform such as control of their own resources and better prices for their commodity exports.

Little response was made to the demands of the Group of 77. Meanwhile, the North was beginning to experience the impact of changing conditions. Trade deficits and rising prices confronted the United States. It was becoming obvious that shortages of certain resources were inevitable.

Food and fuel became the weapons of confrontation in the early 1970s. As the economic battle intensified, the South began to renew its demands for significant reforms in the international economic order. Finally, a special session of the United Nations was requested. It was convened in April 1974.

The Sixth Special Session. Special sessions of the United Nations are unusual. It was even more unusual that the Sixth Special Session dealt with the economic matters of "Raw Materials and Development." The session became the sounding board for many repressed hostilities and ended on a strong confrontative note. Particularly significant was the fact that the Third World came to the session with a new image of its own bargaining power, primarily as a result of the recent successes of OPEC.

The major action of the Sixth Special Session was the passage of resolutions on the "Establishment of a New International Economic Order." The resolutions, which were opposed by the United States and several other developed countries, contained a number of proposals that the Southern bloc had been supporting for years. These included the right to nationalize foreign-owned property without paying full compensation, the endorsement of OPEC-like alliances, the removal of tariffs, commodity agreements, and the transfer of technology from the North to the South. United States policy began to shift after a confrontation in April, 1975.

The Seventh Special Session. Soon afterward, the United States began to take seriously the bargaining strength of the South and to formulate positions that reflected this new evaluation of the international scene. This change was made dramatically evident when Secretary of State Kissinger's speech was delivered at the beginning of the Seventh Special Session. The speech contained a package of proposals that were conciliatory enough to Third World demands that they became the focal point of the Session. Also, moderate leadership in the Group of 77 asserted itself, creating a climate of mutual dialogue and cooperation. A final resolution on "Development and International Cooperation" was passed unanimously, with the United States recording "reservations" about certain provisions.

Agreement was reached on proposals to increase research on food production and to increase monetary support for the International Fund for Agricultural Development and the World Food Conference. Progress was made in such areas as withdrawal of tariff restrictions, commodity price stabilization, and development aid goals. Much was left unresolved, but at least a dialogue was begun that offers some hope for future progress.

Third World Responsibilities

The Third World must make firm commitments to seeing that all people share in the benefits that are derived from development efforts. In many cases the ruling class in the Third World is even less committed to human equality than is the developed world. They have for years controlled power and wealth by keeping the majority of the population uneducated and economically subservient. These ruling minorities control virtually all of the resources and means of wealth, thus locking most people out of any realistic possibility for self-improvement. The crucial factor for self-improvement, which is incentive, is smothered.

Examples of the inequity of wealth and power in underdeveloped countries are numerous. In El Salvador, one-third of the wealth is controlled by 5 percent of the people.[8] Ninety percent of the land in Ethiopia is controlled by 10 percent of the populace, while in Guatemala .2 percent of the landholders have 40.8 percent of all property.[9] Nor are these examples atypical of the situation in the Third and Fourth Worlds.

The concentration of land ownership is being intensified by large land purchases by international corporations. Such purchases remove land-use control even further from the masses of people.

Land reform in the developing world will be essential before significant progress can be made toward raising the standard of living for most people in these countries. This does not necessarily mean the immediate redistribution of all land. It does mean, however, that at the very least there must be a program of steady redistribution of economic opportunity. The doors to "having a chance" must be unlocked for the great majority of those in the Third and Fourth Worlds.

First World Responsibilities

Just as the developing countries have specific actions they must take, so also do the developed countries. Some of these actions such as trade reform and development philosophy already have been mentioned. Another crucial area, however, where change is needed is in the amount of aid that is made available by developed countries, especially the United States.

The United States has been giving foreign aid for many years. This country has been generous at times, less so at other times. A particular time of generosity was just after World War II when our aid, given to rebuild war-torn Europe, amounted to almost 3 percent of our gross national product.

United States developmental aid is now given under Public Law 480. It is administered by the Agency for International Development. The United States also funnels significant amounts of aid through related international multilateral channels, such as the United Nations Developmental Program and the World Bank. Until recently, military aid and developmental aid were appropriated in the same legislation, thus making it hard at times to know what amount of our aid actually was going into development. However, in the International Development and Food Assistance Act of 1975, Congress separated the two and authorized that economic developmental assistance be a category of its own.

Aid had also been used in recent years as a political weapon. The great bulk of it went to military allies, regardless of need. Congress has now insisted, however, that most developmental aid go to the poorest nations, the Most Seriously Affected nations (MSA's). Congress also has insisted that attention be paid to directing aid to where it can do the most good for the poorest people in the poorest nations. Thus in the authorization bill for fiscal year 1976, the President is required to concentrate the bulk of aid in countries that are making the best efforts in land reform, increased agricultural self-sufficiency, reduced infant mortality, and control of population growth.

Although this nation is at times a generous giver, it is not as generous as many believe. In fact, United States aid has been decreasing proportionately for twenty-five years. In 1974, all United States governmental aid amounted to .25 percent of the gross national product. For every $100 of economic output, 25 cents was given to overseas relief. In 1975, the percentage was .23; in 1976, it is .20; and in 1977, it will be .17.[10] In 1974, disbursements for Overseas Development Assistance were $3.4 billion. In the same year $5.8 billion was spent in the United States for jewelry and watches, $13.8 billion for tobacco products, and $22.9 billion for alcoholic beverages.[11]

The International Strategy for the Second United Nations Development Decade has set a goal of .7 percent of gross national product as the aid goal for developed countries. Nearly all of the Development Assistance Countries (DAC's) have accepted this goal. The United States has not. Nor, as seen above, is this nation even moving in the direction of increasing the percentage of the gross national product going for aid.

Food aid also is falling short of targeted goals. In 1975, world food aid was eight million tons, two million tons short of the target.[12] More than half of the food aid comes from the United States, so United States' action is critical.

It is important to realize that the country giving aid also receives some benefits. First, not everything that goes under the term *development assistance aid* is a gift. More than half of the aid is in the form of loans that must be paid back. Foreign aid also provides a market for United States goods and stimulates the growth of new markets. Some authorities even believe that aid results in the return of more foreign exchange than was invested by way of the aid.[13]

The giving of increased foreign aid demands no significant

sacrifices on the part of the people in developed nations. To reach the goal of .7 percent of our gross national product, only 1.5 percent of new wealth will have to be directed into aid.[14] To reach the goal of the "Right to Food" resolution, however, should be our target. The resolution calls for an increase of development assistance "until such assistance has reached the target of 1 percent of our total national production (GNP)." It affirms that every person has a right to food.

Surely this is not too great a sacrifice to ask of those who already are using up most of the world's resources. And surely such should be but a starting point for Christians who understand that God loves "them" just as he loves "us."

Personal Responsibilities

What do I have to do with global justice? That is a good question. Obviously it is difficult to grasp the implications of global justice for the individual. Here are some suggestions for possible response.

1. *Awareness of foreign missions.* Christians are concerned about extending the message of Jesus Christ to the ends of the earth (Matt. 28:19-20). We cannot be interested in sharing the gospel message in all lands unless we care about world hunger.

2. *Appreciation of world religions.* Christians need to understand mankind's groping for God and all the shapes this search takes (Rom. 1:20; 2:14-15). We must be sensitive to the keen consciences of those who have never heard the gospel.

3. *Openness to internationals.* As we open our own homes and lives to the many persons from other lands who live and study in the United States, it is possible for us to identify more readily and sincerely with the hunger and hurt that many of them have known. Warm hospitality is a Christian grace (Heb. 13:1-2).

4. *Acknowledgment of our own racism.* Most of us need to deal with the institutional and cultural racism that has infected

us from our early childhood. To offer our condemnation of the poor and hungry grows out of a prejudice against anyone different from us (Jas. 2:9). There is a parallel to racism that could be called *poorism*.

5. *Development of world awareness.* Keeping up with the news should mean more than watching reports of the latest armed robberies, car wrecks, and rapes on television just before bedtime. Christians have a moral obligation to stay abreast of developments in other lands. We need to know and care about the earthquake in China as well as the murder on the other side of town.

6. *Acceptance of global citizenship.* As we become increasingly informed of the events of our world, we begin to see our oneness with all mankind and the necessity of assuming our role as world citizens. After all, God has made of one blood all nations of men dwelling on the face of the earth (Acts 17:26).

7. *Opposition to national idolatry.* There is a form of civil religion that equates Americanism with Christianity. This is sin. God alone is worthy of worship. One guilty of narrow nationalism refuses to do his part in the world hunger crisis.

8. *Affirmation of international cooperation.* There is a desperate need for international forums for communication and cooperation on world problems. The United Nations and similar organizations play vital roles in the maintenance of peace and the advancement of cooperation.

9. *Rejection of militarism.* It is entirely possible that the only way strong nations can meet the needs of hungry people is with plowshares made from swords and pruning hooks fashioned from spears (Mic. 4:3). Christians have a positive responsibility to make peace, not war.

10. *Involvement in the political process.* Global justice questions are faced on a governmental level, not an individual level. Christians have an awesome responsibility to work for justice

in governmental decisions affecting all mankind.

Most of us grew up with a mother who hovered over us insisting: "Eat every bit of that food on your plate. Just think of all the hungry children in China who would like to have that food you're wasting." Maybe Mother was closer to being right than we are willing to admit.

For Thought and Discussion

1. What is the relationship between Christian commitment and citizenship responsibility? How can Christian concern about world hunger be expressed by political action?

2. What are the dominant characteristics of the present international scene as described in this chapter? What role has our nation played in each of these factors?

3. Recount the recent changes in international relationships. How have alliances like OPEC affected the developing countries?

4. What responsibility does the Third World have toward helping alleviate world hunger? What responsibilities do the First World countries have concerning this issue?

5. What can you do about global justice? What actions do you plan to take immediately? How can you get others involved? What can you urge your church to do?

9
OK, Where Do I Start?

A Fable

They were not overdressed, but their clothes spoke of quality, impeccable with a hint of flair—the right balance for the morning's gathering. On this fall Sunday the four of them had just come from morning worship service at their church in the near suburbs.

One of the couples seemed in their mid-twenties, at that point where youthful enthusiasm has merged with the air of confidence from early business success. Their companions appeared in the prime of middle age, reflecting a subdued pride of accomplishment mixed with physical well-being born of careful diet and measured exertion.

They had chosen a restaurant table near, but not next to, the tinted window, a location affording a view without distraction. After suitable study of the oversized menu, featuring samples in four-color views, each husband placed an order. In due course the diners were enjoying the cuisine, paced with relaxed conversation. They murmured proper appreciation of the dishes set before them, each laden with ample serving.

The young wife saw them first. Perhaps the two youngsters had left their customary alley route for a short cut beside the eating place. Maybe some movement among the diners caught the children's notice. Or the seductive aroma may have beckoned them. Whatever the reason, there they were, faces pressed to the window. They said nothing to each other, but stared at the tastefully set tables, the finely dressed patrons, and the heaping servings.

The pair's color was uncertain. Perhaps brown; or black. A generous trimming of grime on each face blurred the hue. Their skin matched their clothes, dirty with a thoroughness achieved only over many days. They were not exactly thin, but their gaunt faces and the dullness in their eyes hinted at a lack of proper food.

The young wife stared, saying nothing. The sudden lump in her throat, born of a surge of pity, blocked words. She gently laid down her food-laden fork, but its soft tap against the plate drew the attention of the others at the table. Without a spoken question, they followed her line of sight. And they, too, became arrested by the sad tableau at the window.

Perhaps a dozen thoughts scampered through the young woman's mind. Among them were words she vaguely associated with the morning's sermon. The message, she seemed to recall, had something to do with responsibility to neighbors.

Her husband broke the silence. "Seeing those hungry faces makes this steak taste a little flat," he ventured. The older man nodded his agreement. His wife added, "They look so helpless."

The younger woman found her voice. Gazing sternly at her companions, she demanded, "How can you look at them and not do something?"

"What can we do? challenged her husband.

"It's so simple, so obvious," she answered with disdain, looking from the still-steaming food to the hungry eyes.

She pushed back from the table. With an unaccustomed directness she strode almost silently across the carpet. Straight to the window she moved, found the tassled cord dangling at the wall, and firmly pulled it. With only a sibilant swish the heavy, almost luxurious, drapery material shut out the view. The drapes swayed for a moment before their weight stilled the motion.

Resuming her seat, the young woman reached for her fork. "There now," she said brightly, "isn't that much better?"[1]

Perhaps the fable is more appealing to us than we would care to admit. The horror of world hunger is a scene none of us chooses to gaze upon. The temptation to close the curtain is especially strong when the need we confront is related so directly to us and our way of life.

The agony of this book has been to draw back the curtain on a scene that demands response from each of us. Whether we realize it or not, whether we like it or not, we are part and parcel of the problem identified as world hunger. It is our issue. This chapter is dedicated to the "response-ability" of every reader. The suggestions made here are starters, stepping-stones to move us along the path of involvement with the world hunger crisis. Such involvement seeks genuinely to meet the needs of all persons concerned and is a direct evidence of the authenticity of our Christian commitment.

Dean Freudenberger and Paul Minus in their excellent book *Christian Responsibility in a Hungry World* diagram a procedure for response that includes increasing activity in various areas of concern.[2]

INCREASING SCOPE OF RESPONSE

INCREASING INTENSITY OF RESPONSE ↓	HEIGHTENING AWARENESS	MOBILIZING CHURCH RESOURCES	DEVELOPING RESPONSIBLE LIFE-STYLES	REORDERING PUBLIC PRIORITIES
STEP 1— A BEGINNING				
STEP 2— A LITTLE MORE				
STEP 3— STILL MORE				
STEP 4— MUCH MORE				

The grid offers a reminder of a need for balance in the areas of response to world hunger. At the same time it challenges every person or group to find a beginning point and move to more advanced response. Freudenberger and Minus devote four chapters to developing the divisions of the diagram. These categories will serve as the subdivisions of this chapter and general guidelines for directing our response to world hunger.

Heightening Awareness

A successful approach to dealing with any issue involves an increasing awareness of the dimensions of the problem being considered. As this book tries to point out, the world hunger crisis is a multifaceted problem. In order to accomplish the goal of increased awareness on your part as an individual and on the part of others, several steps should be followed.

After the topic has been clarified, such as world hunger, gather as much factual information as possible. Study books and periodicals that relate to the subject. A list of excellent books concerning world hunger can be found at the conclusion of this book. Contact organizations that work on the problem. A list of such organizations concerned with world hunger is contained under the "Mobilizing Church Resources" and "Reordering Public Priorities" sections of this chapter.

Once the basic information has been gathered, study intensively the material. Any good student must do his homework! You probably will find an overlapping of basic information, and this information you must consider. It is also important to update your knowledge by keeping up with the latest available information.

As you begin to determine the basic direction of the information you have gathered, relate your understanding of the Christian faith to the topic. For example, the Bible tells us that God created all persons in his image. This doctrine emphasizes the inherent worth of every individual and forms the theological basis for our understanding that all persons are equal. The Bible also tells us that God is love. His love is not a sentimental emotion but an active, even aggressive, love that seeks the best for all persons even at expense of self. Jesus dramatically demonstrated his love when he gave his life for all persons. The Bible goes on to tell us that Christian people are to be channels through whom the love of God can be actualized in every generation and to every person.

These doctrines give us direction and encouragement as we begin to relate them to such problems as world hunger. We realize that the starving person in Bangladesh or Upper Volta has the same worth as we do and, therefore, is entitled to the same basic rights, most certainly including the right to food. We also understand that because God loves every person with his unlimited love, and we are agents of that love, then we must give of our abundance to those who are without adequate necessities for life. Jesus said we are to give more than is requested even if it means the "shirt off our back."

Applying one's faith to the issues of the day is necessary to vital Christian involvement. Christian theological insights offer powerful motivation as we seek to meet human need. The application of Christian doctrines to the issue of world hunger provides us with a concern that is more than humanitarian motivation; it is a divine imperative for our lives.

Once we begin to understand the issue from a factual and a theological basis, we are ready to begin to draw conclusions. These conclusions must be in harmony with the best insights available from our study and our faith. In drawing conclusions, one must be careful to avoid extreme solutions or simplistic answers such as triage. Both extremism and simiplicity ignore the complexity of issues. One would make a mistake to suggest solutions to the world hunger crisis that border on the extreme or overly simple.

This process of gathering information, researching the topic, applying Christian insights, and drawing conclusions can be either an individualistic experience or a group participation experience. Either way the result ought to be an increased awareness of the problem and a concern that leads to effective action. Information alone is never the final goal for Christian concern related to social issues; it must always lead to decisive activity designed to help alleviate the problem.

Once the process is completed, it is vitally important to share the information and conclusions with others. Motivating other persons to active involvement is part of heightening awareness.

Mobilizing Church Resources

The Christian community has much to offer when it comes to dealing with urgent human concerns like world hunger. There are denominational and interdenominational agencies whose primary task is combatting world hunger. These agencies provide a channel through which monies can be given and translated directly into relief and development projects.

The advantage of these church agencies as opposed to government-sponsored relief is outlined by Larry Minear. He notes that church-related relief organizations' "involvement with people at the grass roots level lessens some of the political and bureaucratic entanglements." They also have "greater freedom than do governments." In addition, these organizations "tap into the networks of relationships already existing in developing countries." And finally, their "broad independence from the United States government frees them to respond to human need where it exists."[3]

Examples of denominational organizations that have been vitally involved in hunger relief and development projects include Lutheran World Relief, Catholic Relief Services, and the Foreign Mission Board of the Southern Baptist Convention. These agencies have excellent records in regard to their stewardship of the money given them for world hunger. Because of the existing structure and field staffs of these organizations, they have been able to use directly for world hunger over ninety cents out of every dollar contributed. Due to bureaucratic overhead expenses, governmental and secular organizations, on the other hand, often deliver less than half this percentage to actual hunger relief projects.

Interdenominational agencies that have done outstanding work in the cause of world hunger include Church World Service, CROP, Agricultural Missions Foundation, Ltd., and World Vision International. Addresses for these and other agencies are included in Appendix B of this book. CARE is a private relief organization whose effectiveness and responsibility in regard to world hunger concerns are above question.

As Christian people are becoming increasingly involved in the world hunger crisis, so their churches reflect their involvement. Many churches have taken concrete action. The First Baptist Church of Houston, Texas, has designated 1 percent of their total church budget for world hunger. Other churches are taking designated offerings to go to their relief agencies. Some churches are adopting covenants which affirm Christian participation in world hunger relief.

Every church can be involved in meeting world hunger needs. Study groups can use this book and others to survey the issue of world hunger. Specific action can be taken. Churches can encourage their membership to contribute to world hunger relief through their own channels or to other agencies.

Churches also can sponsor special events that serve to create public awareness of the world hunger issue. Such events as a public forum, a "hunger dinner" in which a typical poverty meal is served, a fast day, a hunger walk have been used by church groups.

However it is accomplished, Christians have many outlets for their concern for people victimized by world hunger. As church resources are mobilized into action, hungry people can be fed.

Developing Responsible Life-styles

Eventually, response to the world hunger crisis must take place on an individual and family basis. As has been made clear in previous chapters, one of the reasons for the food crisis is that we in the developed countries have consumed more than our fair share. We in the United States and Canada, who are 6 percent of the world's population, cannot go on consuming 40 percent of the earth's resources and expect world hunger to go away. It just will not happen. We must begin to do our part to reduce our consumption pattern as a part of the war on hunger.

Many suggestions concerning the simplification of life-style could be made. Here is a list to help you get started.

—Be responsible and conservative in planning meals for your family.

—Reduce your consumption of meat, especially grain-fed fatty meats. Eliminating massive amounts of meat from our meals helps not only the hungry but also ourselves. There is now a near consensus among doctors on the contributive role of animal fats to heart disease.[4]

—Substitute vegetable protein for animal protein. The American Heart Association emphasizes that for personal health Americans should cut their meat consumption by one third.

—When you buy beef, buy only grass-fed beef. Grass-fed beef permits the conversion of vast quantities of roughage on land that is not suitable for the raising of crops into a high quality, much sought-after protein product. Cattle fed on grass in grazing areas require no grain, but those on feedlots consume about ten pounds of grain for every pound of meat added.[6]

—Utilize cookbooks that contain recipes for well-balanced diets that cut down on waste and make the most of high protein, meatless meals (see Bibliography).

—Reduce or eliminate consumption of "junk foods." Do away with the low food value, high calorie products such as potato chips, sugared soft drinks, candy, etc. In 1974, Americans spent more than $670 million on chewing gum alone, averaging 175 pieces of gum per person per year![7]

—Eliminate wastefulness. Adopt the policy "use it up, wear it out, make it do, or do without."

—Do not throw away food. Make creative use of leftovers. Take excess restaurant food home with you.

—Recycle everything that is reusable. Some churches serve as collection centers for recyclable materials.

—Grow your own garden. Your food will taste better, and it will help alleviate the strain on the world food market.

—Feed pets table scraps instead of commercial pet foods that contain foodstuffs edible by human beings. Americans spend $2.5 million on commercially prepared pet food—more than six times the amount they spend on baby food and more than enough to nourish the one third of the world's population that goes hungry.[8]

—Have your pet sterilized. Or do not have a pet at all. Agriculture Secretary Earl Butz has stated that Americans could help feed hungry people by reducing our dog and cat population by 50 percent.[9]

—Decrease or eliminate the use of commercial fertilizer on your lawn. Consider contributing to world hunger relief the amount you spend on yard maintenance.

—Reduce your consumption of gasoline and other forms of energy. Ten gallons of gasoline, which an average Western citizen uses in one month of pleasure driving, is sufficient to produce the food necessary for the survival of one adult.[10]

—Skip at least one meal a week and contribute the average cost of that meal to world hunger relief.

—Try living on a poverty allowance (16 cents per meal) for a week or longer.

—Practice fasting as another way of knowing what it means to be hungry.

—Oppose the use of grains for brewing beer and whiskey. In 1973, American distillers used 1.1 million tons of grain to produce 183 million gallons of whiskey, and American brewers used 3 million tons of grain to produce 4.6 billion gallons of beer. This 4.1 million tons of grain is enough to have fed 20 million people for one year on a minimal adequate diet.[11] Another way to say it is, "Have a drink, starve a child."

—Support the movement to grow food for the hungry on land that is now being used to grow tobacco.

—Encourage your church to make a continued emphasis on the world hunger problem. Urge your church to be responsible and conservative in its meal planning.

—Give sacrificially on the behalf of the poor. Seriously consider giving a graduated tithe of your income. A graduated tithe means that as your income increases, you increase the percentage of your giving. A portion of this increase could be designated for world hunger relief through your denominational organization, such as the Foreign Mission Board of the Southern Baptist Convention.

—Understand that a genuine commitment to world missions necessitates participation in world hunger relief. The sharing of bread prepares for the word of grace.

—Stay informed about and sensitive to human needs in the world.

—Pray.

The final suggestion is in the form of a question to be continually asked. "Is my life and life-style contributing to or alleviating the hunger in our world today?" Only you can answer.

Reordering Public Priorities

Response to the world hunger crisis is not complete without effective citizenship action. As we begin to see ourselves as world citizens caring for the peoples of this planet, we must help shape public policy accordingly.

We must participate in reordering public policies because many decisions made by our government vitally affect the physical destiny of thousands of persons. Public policies on issues such as international trade, aid, agricultural production, economics, energy, and military expenditures are crucial to the very existence of many of the world's people. Inadequate, irresponsible or self-serving action by our government has tragic human consequences. The only way we can make a difference in these complex and massive processes is by functioning effectively as citizens.

As we seek to fulfill our citizenship responsibility, there are several organizations that can be helpful. Bread for the World is an effective citizens' lobby for the world's hungry. Based in New York City, Bread for the World is a Christian organization that seeks to influence United States public policy on issues directly related to world hunger. Responsible and reliable information on important hunger-related legislation can be obtained in its monthly newsletter to members. Memberships in Bread for the World are available at the cost of ten dollars per year. The address is;

Bread for the World
235 East 49th Street
New York, New York 10017

Another important information source is the Overseas Development Council (ODC). ODC is a reliable source for hard data on complex economic and social issues. It is a respected research group that provides vital information on United States relations to the rest of the world. Information can be obtained from ODC by writing:

Overseas Development Council
1717 Massachusetts Avenue, N.W.
Washington, D.C. 20036

As information is gathered on United States public policy and pending legislation is analyzed as to its effect on the world's hungry people, it is vitally important to communicate with your govenment officials. Elected officials in Washington may be contacted at these addresses and telephones.

By mail/telegram/mailgram:

Congressperson ______
U.S. House of Representatives
Washington, D.C. 20515

Senator ______
U.S. Senate
Washington, D.C. 20510

President ______
The White House
Washington, D.C. 20500

Mailgrams are $2.00 for 100 words, delivered the next day. Personal opinion message telegram is $2.00 for 15 words, same day. Call local Western Union office for both.

By phone: House or Senate members: 202/224-3121; White House: 202/456-1414.

You can obtain a list of members on key House and Senate committees, as well as a state-by-state roster of the House and Senate, by writing Bread for the World.

As letters are written to public servants, it is important to keep several points in mind Be concise, factual, logical, and clear. Rambling, lengthy letters will not be read. It is, of course, vitally important to be Christian. Threatening letters are self-defeating.

As we work together in communicating with our elected representatives, we can influence American public policy in a way that helps meet human need. That is being a good citizen.

Conclusion

As we increasingly become involved in the world hunger crisis, we must seek wisdom to guide us. E. F. Schumacher has well described the importance of genuine wisdom as we face life and death issues.

But what is wisdom? Where can it be found? Here we come to the crux of the matter: it can be read about in numerous publications but it can be *found* only inside oneself. To be able to find it, one has first to liberate oneself from such masters as greed and envy. The stillness following liberation—even if only momentary—produces the insights of wisdom which are obtainable in no other way.

They enable us to see the hollowness and fundamental unsatisfactoriness of a life devoted primarily to the pursuit of material ends, to the neglect of the spiritual. Such a life necessarily sets man against man and nation against nation, because man's needs are infinite and infinitude can be achieved only in the spiritual realm, never in the material. Man assuredly needs to rise above this humdrum 'world'; wisdom shows him the way to do it; without wisdom, he is driven to build up a monster economy, which destroys the world, and to seek fantastic satisfactions, like landing a man on the moon. Instead of overcoming the 'world' by moving towards saintliness, he tries to overcome it by gaining preeminence in wealth, power, science, or indeed any imaginable 'sport'.[12]

Jesus said, "Be of good cheer, I have overcome the world." And so it must be with those of us who claim his name as we live in this world of need.

For Thought and Discussion

1. How did the fable at the start of this chapter affect you? Put yourself in the place of the children and discuss the effect of the closed drape on you.

2. How can you help other persons become aware of the world hunger problem? What other persons or groups are concerned about the problem? How can you work together?

3. What is your church doing concerning world hunger? What else could it do? How can you get additional efforts started?

4. How does the way we live affect the hunger crisis? What do you plan to do about it?

5. How can practicing active citizenship help relieve world hunger? What specific actions can you take to influence governmental action? Outline your plan of action.

Appendix A: Answers to Objections

1. *What does feeding the hungry have to do with the Great Commission?*

Matthew 28:19-20 indicates that as we are going to all nations discipling them, we are to "teach them to observe all that I have commanded you." Our Lord vividly taught us, both in words and in actions, that we are to feed the hungry. If we do not obey this clear commandment of our Lord, then why should those whom we are trying to disciple obey him at all?

2. *How do you explain the Scripture passage that says "the poor you have with you always?"*

Jesus' comment in Matthew 26:11 concerning the poor was not meant to contradict the strong responsibility to the impoverished taught in Matthew 25:31-40, but rather was intended to rebuke the self-righteousness of his own disciples. His answer, which is actually a restatement of Deuteronomy 15:11, emphasizes that the consistent presence of the poor presents a continuing opportunity for ministry and a burden of responsibility to the genuine Christian.

3. *Shouldn't we take care of our own hungry first?*

The focusing of attention on the hungry of the world ought to make us more sensitive to those who are hungry right around us and to the waste of our own abundance. Christian compassion and ministry, although it may begin in Jerusalem always radiates out to the "ends of the world."

4. *America can't feed the world; haven't we already done more than any other nation?*

Although it may be true that America cannot feed the world by itself and that much has been done in the past, it is still true that as 6 percent of the world's people we consume over 40 percent of the world's resources. We must honestly face our Lord's words in Luke 12:48: "To whom much is given, of him will much be required" (RSV).

5. *Does our aid ever really get to the hungry people anyway?*
While about 20 percent of the grain shipped by our government to needy countries is lost to rats and spoilage and more is lost to thievery and corruption, even 50 percent of additional aid is better than none at all. However, grain and moneys given through church channels go directly, without loss, to the starving people through our missionaries. This enables them to give a "cup of cold water in Jesus' name," thereby validating the message they proclaim.

6. *I'm just one person; what can I do?*
Individual action is the starting point for all great movements. What you do combined with the response of other Christians produces a result that is more than the sum of the participants' action. Because the action of one stimulates the awareness and creativity of another and they in turn effect response in still others, the process is one of multiplication and not simply addition. It is working on the principle that God is at work in us yielding results more than our capacity (John 14:12).

7. *Doesn't our aid to the hungry just perpetuate the hunger crisis?*
While some may coldly calculate the facts of starvation and advise that we must "let nature take its course," the Christian who takes the Bible seriously could never subscribe to that view. Inherent to the gospel we proclaim is the cardinal belief that every person is made in God's image and bought by the blood of our Lord and, therefore, is of supreme value to our Father and to us. To let a fellow human starve is unthinkable, unchristian and unbiblical (Jas. 2:15-17).

8. If people would help themselves, such as eating the sacred cows in India, wouldn't that solve the problem?

While pagan practices can never be condoned as just by the Christian, our role is not to seek to justify our inaction because of their errors. For the caring Christian, there can be no excuse that will permit our consciences to be at peace if we allow millions to starve without any decisive action on our part (Rom. 14:12).

9. *Anybody can survive if they just work, can't they?*
The vast majority of the predicted deaths by starvation will be children five years of age and under—many of them homeless. The effect of an inadequate diet is an inability to move one's muscles because they are being consumed as protein by the person's own body. In light of these facts it seems that the Christian has a clear responsibility to the oppressed and wretched.

10. *If they'd just practice birth control, wouldn't that solve the problem?*
While a major factor in the world food crisis is population growth, there are many other causes, not the least of which is the comparatively high affluence in which you and I live. Before we blame others and thereby seek to absolve ourselves of any responsibility, we must hear the implication of our Lord's statement in John 8:7, "Let him who is without sin among you be the first to throw a stone" (RSV).

11. *Isn't this hunger crisis and famine just a sign of the Lord's return that the Bible predicts and a work of the judgment of God?*
If so, then in preparation for the judgment, we had better be part of the sheep who are feeding the hungry rather than the goats who are gorging themselves (Matt. 25:31-46).

Appendix B: Resources

Africare.

Address: 1424 - 16th Street, N.W., Washington, D.C. 20036.

Agricultural Missions, Inc.

Address: 475 Riverside Drive, New York, New York 10027.

Related to National Council of Churches.

Agricultural Missions Foundation, Ltd.

Address: P. O. Box 388, Yazoo City, Mississippi 39194.

American Freedom from Hunger Foundation.

Address: 1625 "I" Street, Washington, D.C. 20036.

Information and fund raising organization. Some materials available on request.

Bread for the World.

Address: 235 East 49th Street, New York, New York 10017.

Seeks from a Christian perspective to influence U.S. policy on hunger. Regular newsletter is available, along with other pamphlets.

CARE, Inc.

Address: 660 First Avenue, New York, New York 10016.

Catholic Relief Services.

Address: 1011 First Avenue, New York, New York 10022.

Church World Service.

Address: 475 Riverside Drive, New York, New York 10027

Council on Religion and International Affairs (CRIA).

Address: 170 East 64th Street, New York, New York 10021.

Seeks to apply religious ethics to international issues. Publishes *Worldview* plus various other studies.

CROP.

Address: Box 968, Elkhart, Indiana 46514.

Foreign Mission Board of the Southern Baptist Convention, World Hunger Fund.

Address: P. O. Box 6597, 3806 Monument Avenue, Richmond, Virginia 23230.

Friends Committee on National Legislation.

Address: 245 Second Street, N.E., Washington, D.C. 20002. Regular newsletter called *The Washington Newsletter* is available. Well-respected for accurate political information.

IMPACT.

Address: 110 Maryland Avenue, N.E., Washington, D.C. 20002. Interfaith network to inform citizens concerning public issues. Works closely with Washington Interreligious Staff Council. Current political information available.

Interreligious Task Force on U.S. Food Policy.

Address: 100 Maryland Avenue, N.E., Washington, D.C. 20002. Excellent background and current information on political issues which relate to U.S. food policy.

Lutheran World Relief.

Address: 315 Park Avenue, South, New York, New York 10010.

Network.

Address: 224 "D" Street, S.E., Washington, D.C. 20005

A Catholic group committed to social justice. Good political information on hunger issues.

Overseas Development Council.

Address: 1717 Massachusetts Avenue, N.W., Washington, D.C. 20036. A respected research group that speaks to policy makers and others. Responsible research continually being made available.

Oxfam-America.

Address: 302 Columbus Avenue, Boston, Massachusetts 02116.

United Nations.

The U.N. has several organizations which relate in some way to world hunger. There is a general U.N. Information Center at 1028 Connecticut Avenue, N.W., Washington, D.C. 20006.

World Vision International.

Address: 912 West Huntington Drive, Monrovia, California 91016.

World Watch Institute.

Address: 1776 Massachusetts Avenue, N.W., Washington, D.C. 20036. Research group committed to early identification of and policy discussion about emerging international issues.

Notes

Chapter 1: Can You Show Me a Picture of Hunger?

1. Peter Stoler, "How Hunger Kills," *Time*, November 11, 1974, p. 68.
2. *Post-American*, February-March, 1974, p. 4.
3. Lester R. Brown and Erik P. Eckholm, *By Bread Alone* (New York: Praeger Publishers, 1974), p. 30.
4. Stanley Mooneyham, *What do you say to a hungry world?* (Waco, Texas: Word Books, 1975), pp. 48-49.
5. Brown and Eckholm, *By Bread Alone*, p. 26.
6. Mooneyham, *What do you say to a hungry world?*, p. 75.
7. Stoler, "How Hunger Kills," p. 68.
8. *Center Survey*, January 15, 1974, p. 2.
9. Brown and Eckholm, *By Bread Alone*, pp. 29-30.
10. *Time*, April 8, 1974, p. 40.
11. Jane F. Brody, *New York Times*, October 11, 1974.
12. Brown and Eckholm, *By Bread Alone*, p. 12.
13. Personal journal of Phil Strickland, p. 4.
14. Mooneyham, *What do you say to a hungry world?*, p. 113.
15. *IFCO News*, July-August 1974, p. 5.
16. Personal journal of Phil Strickland, pp. 2-3.
17. Nevin S. Scrimshaw. Personal presentation to the Conference on Food and Population sponsored by *The Conference Board* in Dallas, Texas, May, 1975.
18. "Running Out of Food?" *Newsweek*, November 11, 1974, p. 60.

Chapter 2: You Mean There's a Verse in the Bible About Bangladesh?

1. All Scripture quotations in this chapter are from the *New American Standard Bible*.
2. C. Dean Freudenberger and Paul M. Minus, Jr., *Christian Responsibility in a Hungry World* (Nashville: Abingdon, 1976), p. 40.
3. *Ibid.*, pp. 41-42.

Chapter 3: What Does Theology Have to do With Bloated Bellies?

1. *Mary Knoll* magazine, June 1971, p. 37.
2. *Saturday Review*, March 8, 1975, p. 4.

3. T. B. Maston, *Why Live the Christian Life*? (Nashville: Thomas Nelson Inc., 1974), p. 170.

4. Robert L. Heilbroner, *An Inquiry Into the Human Prospect* (New York: W. W. Norton and Company Inc., 1975), p. 169.

Chapter 4: WHAT WOULD MOVE ME TO HELP HUNGRY PEOPLE?

1. Martin Luther King, Jr., *Strength to Love* (New York: Pocket Books, 1963), p. 168.

2. Amos N. Wilder, *Otherworldliness and the New Testament* (New York: Harper and Brothers, 1954), p. 19.

3. Dietrich Bonhoeffer, *Ethics* (London: SCM Press Ltd., 1960), p. 95.

4. Georgia Harkness, *Christian Ethics* (New York: Abingdon Press, 1957), p. 71.

5. Martin Luther, *A Commentary on St. Paul's Epistle to the Galatians,* trans. Theodore Graebner (Grand Rapids: Zondervan Publishing House, n.d.), p. 218.

6. *Ibid*., p. 215.

7. Barbara Ward, "A New Creation? Reflections on the Environmental Issue," in *The Patriot's Bible*, ed. John Eagleson and Philip Scharper (New York: Orbis Books, 1975), p. 70.

Chapter 5: WHO EMPTIED THE CUPBOARD?

1. Roger D. Hansen, ed., *The U.S. and World Development: Agenda for Action* (New York: Praeger Publishers, Inc., 1976), p. 6.

2. James W. Howe, ed., *The U.S. and World Development: Agenda for Action* (New York: Praeger Publishers, Inc., 1975), p. 166.

3. Mooneyham, *What do you say to a hungry world?*, p. 212.

4. Robert S. McNamara, "Address to the Board of Governors," September 1, 1975 (Washington, D.C.: World Bank, 1975), pp. 3-4.

5. Mahbub ul Haq, "The Crisis in Development Strategies," *Anticipation 12* (September 1972), p. 3, quoted in Mooneyham, *What do you say to a hungry world?*, p. 214.

6. Arthur Simon, *Bread for the World* (New York: Paulist Press; Grand Rapids, Michigan: Wm. B. Eerdmans, 1975), p. 9.

7. Hansen, *The U.S. and World Development; Agenda for Action*, 1976, pp. 156-58.

8. Mooneyham, *What do you say to a hungry world?*, pp. 79-80.

9. *Malthus and America*, A Report About Food and People by the Subcommittee on Department Operations of the Committee on Agriculture, House of Representatives (Washington, D.C.: U.S. Government Printing Office, 1974), p. 5.

10. Hansen, *The U.S. and World Development: Agenda for Action*, 1976, p. 85.

11. Frances Moore Lappé, "Fantasies of Famine." *Harper's*, February 1975.

12. Simon, *Bread for the World*, p. 6.
13. Brown and Eckholm, *By Bread Alone*, p. 242.
14. Hansen, *The U.S. and World Development: Agenda for Action*, 1976, 162.
15. Pierre Pradervand, "The Neo-Malthusian Myth," *African Report*, July-August 1974, p. 34, quoted in Mooneyham, *What do you say to a hungry world?*, p. 146.
16. Marvin E. Wolfgang, ed., "Adjusting to Scarcity," *Annals of the American Academy of Political and Social Science* 420 (July 1975):2.
17. Brown and Eckholm, *By Bread Alone*, p. 181.
18. "1975 World Population Data Sheet" (Washington, D.C.: Population Reference Bureau, 1975).
19. Heilbroner, *An Inquiry into the Human Prospect*, p. 35.
20. Brown and Eckholm, *By Bread Alone*, p. 44.
21. Mihajlo Mesarovic and Eduard Pestel, *Mankind at the Turning Point: The Second Report to The Club of Rome* (New York: The New American Library, Inc., 1976), p. 80.

Chapter 6: IS THERE A WAY OUT OF THIS MESS?

1. Hansen, *The U.S. and World Development: Agenda for Action*, 1976, p. 68.
2. *Ibid.*
3. Brown and Eckholm, *By Bread Alone*, p. 211.
4. *Ibid.*, p. 214.
5. Susan DeMarco and Susan Sechler, *The Fields Have Turned Brown: Four Essays on World Hunger* (Washington, D.C.: Agribusiness Accountability Project, 1975), p. 64.
6. Mooneyham, *What do you say to a hungry world?*, p. 163.
7. Brown and Eckholm, *By Bread Alone*, p. 156.
8. Mooneyham, *What do you say to a hungry world?*, p. 204.
9. E. F. Schumacher, *Small Is Beautiful: Economics as if People Mattered* (New York: Harper & Row, 1973), p. 186.
10. Mooneyham, *What do you say to a hungry world?*, p. 206.
11. Hansen, *The U.S. and World Development: Agenda for Action*, 1976, p. 15.
12. *Ibid.*, p. 183.
13. *Ibid.*, p. 205.
14. Wes Michaelson, "Interview with Richard Barnet on Multi-National Corporations," *Sojourners*, February 1976, p. 14.

Chapter 7: THE EARTH IS THE LORD'S—OR IS IT?

1. Schumacher, *Small Is Beautiful: Economics as if People Mattered*, p. 127.
2. *Baptist Review*, November-December, 1969, cover.

3. Simon, *Bread for the World*, p. 48.
4. Francis A. Schaeffer, *Pollution and the Death of Man* (Wheaton, Illinois: Tyndale House Publishers, 1970), pp. 91-92.
5. *Ibid.*, p. 89.
6. *Ibid.*, p. 57.
7. Henlee H. Barnette, *The Church and the Ecological Crisis* (Grand Rapids: Wm. B. Eerdmans Publishing Company, 1972), p. 63.

Chapter 8: WHAT DO YOU MEAN, ONE WORLD?
1. Geoffrey Barraclough, "Wealth and Power: The Politics of Food and Oil." *The New York Review of Books*, August 7, 1975, p. 23.
2. Mesarovic and Pestel, *Mankind at the Turning Point: The Second Report to The Club of Rome*, pp. 68-69.
3. *Scientific American*, April, 1975.
4. Paul Simon and Arthur Simon, *The Politics of World Hunger* (New York: Harper's Magazine Press, 1973), p. 185.
5. Simon, *Bread for the World*, p. 128.
6. Dwight D. Eisenhower, "The Chance for Peace," address before The American Society of Newspaper Editors, April 16, 1953.
7. "The United States and the Changing International Economic Order" (IMPACT, Washington, D.C.) No. 4 (April 1976):2.
8. Mooneyham, *What do you say to a hungry world?*, p. 119.
9. *Ibid.*, p. 126.
10. Hansen, *The U.S. and World Development: Agenda for Action*, 1976, p. 203.
11. *Ibid.*, p. 208.
12. *Ibid.*, p. 74.
13. Mooneyham, *What do you say to a hungry world?*, p. 210.
14. *Ibid.*, p. 211.

Chapter 9: OK, WHERE DO I START?
1. Leland F. Webb, *The Commission*, February 1976.
2. Freudenberger and Minus, *Christian Responsibility in a Hungry World*, p. 61.
3. Larry Minear, *New Hope for the Hungry* (New York: Friendship Press, 1975), pp. 96-97.
4. Brown and Eckholm, *By Bread Alone*, p. 200.
5. Boyce Renseberger, "Curb on U.S. Waste Urged to Help World's Hungry," *New York Times*, October 25, 1974.
6. Brown and Eckholm, *By Bread Alone*, p. 205.
7. *New York Times*, October 22, 1975.
8. *Time*, December 23, 1974, p. 58.
9. *Ibid.*

10. Mesarovic and Pestel, *Mankind at the Turning Point: The Second Report to The Club of Rome*, pp. 27-30.

11. Jane F. Brody, "Can Less Drinking Lead to Less Starvation?" *New York Times*, December 11, 1974.

12. Schumacher, *Small Is Beautiful: Economics as if People Mattered*, p. 35.

Selected Bibliography

Brown, Lester R., and Eckholm, Erik P. *By Bread Alone.* New York: Praeger Publishers, 1974.

Paperback. Cost: $3.95. One of the best books available on world hunger. Clear analysis and easy reading.

Commoner, Barry. *The Closing Circle.* New York: Bantam, 1976.

Stresses the interdependence of all people, nations and "systems" and warns of the consequences to be expected if we refuse to face that interdependence.

DeMarco, Susan, and Sechler, Susan. *The Fields Have Turned Brown: Four Essays on World Hunger.* Washington D.C.: Agribusiness Accountability Project, 1975.

No charge. This report contains four essays which deal poignantly with United States trade and aid policies and the green revolution.

Freudenberger, C. Dean, and Minus, Paul M., Jr. *Christian Responsibility in a Hungry World.* Nashville: Abingdon, 1976.

This book by two Methodist professors of theology describes the hunger crisis in detail and offers four chapters of specific suggestions for response. The cost is $2.50.

Global Justice and Development: Report of the Aspen Interreligious Consultation. Washington, D.C.: Overseas Development Council, 1975.

Paperback. Cost: $2.50. A collection of excellent presentations, some fairly technical, on problems and ethics of international justice and development. Excellent section on resources, agencies and statements by religious groups.

Hansen, Roger D., ed. *The U.S. and World Development: Agenda for Action.* New York: Praeger, 1976.

Paperback. Cost: $4.25. Collection of essays that gives an excellent and somewhat technical overview of international relations, development and trade and how they affect world hunger.

Lappé, Frances Moore. *Diet for a Small Planet.* New York: Ballentine Books, 1971.

A critical examination of the inefficient and wasteful use of food to which Americans have become habitually conditioned. It calls for all concerned persons to a responsible pattern of protein consumption through better nutrition and improved diet (with nutrition guide and many recipes).

Longacre, Doris Janzen. *More-with-Less Cookbook.* Scottdale, Pennsylvania: Herald Press, 1976.

A product of Mennonite stewardship, *Cookbook* includes 500 recipes designed to help Christians eat better while consuming less of the world's food resources. It is for those who have determined to eat and spend 10 percent less on food. $4.95, wirebound.

Mooneyham, W. Stanley. *What do you say to a hungry world?* Waco, Texas: Word Books, 1975.

Cost: $6.95. From a distinctly evangelical perspective and in language to which churchmen are accustomed. Offers valuable insights into world hunger.

Schumacher, E. F. *Small Is Beautiful: Economics as if People Mattered.* New York: Harper & Row, 1973.

Paperback. Cost: $3.75. A penetrating examination of economic philosophy written in a down-to-earth manner. The worth of human beings is put above economic progression. A book on economics that makes sense.

Simon, Arthur. *Bread for the World.* New York: Paulist Press; Grand Rapids, Michigan: Wm. B. Eerdmans, 1975.

Paperback. Cost: $1.50. This book is a concise introduction to hunger which focuses on the role of public policy and the necessity of public input concerning those policies.

Sivard, Ruth Leger. *World Military and Social Expenditures 1976.* Leesburg, Virginia: WMSE Publications, 1976.

Contrasts world public spending in the social sector (nutrition, health care, education) with world spending on the arms race, now approaching $300 billion yearly, and analyzes the global implications for the future. Available for $2.50 from WMSE Publications, Box 1003, Leesburg, Virginia 22075.

Taylor, John V. *Enough is Enough.* Naperville, Illinois: SCM Book Club, 1975.

Rejects the growthmania fueling industrialized Western economies and the personal acquisitiveness of so many today. Excess is the common enemy of rich and poor alike, and is to be replaced with distributive justice regarding food and material possessions.

Photo Credits

Page 10–AID, Page 23–David Clanton, Page 39–Bill Clough, Page 49–David Clanton, Page 60–AID, Page 74–David Clanton, Page 90–Larry Jerden, Page 106–David Clanton, and Page 122–Danny Hill, Foreign Mission Board, SBC.

ENDANGERED SPECIES